Designing for

Small Screens

Mobile Phones | Smart Phones

PDAs | Pocket PCs

Navigation Systems

MP3 Players

Game Consoles

Academia
the environment of learning

AVA Publishing SA
Switzerland

An AVA Book
Published by AVA Publishing SA
Rue des Fontenailles 16
Case postale
1000 Lausanne 6
Switzerland
Tel: +41 786 005 109
Email: enquiries@avabooks.ch

Distributed by Thames & Hudson (ex-North America)
181a High Holborn
London WC1V 7QX
United Kingdom
Tel: +44 20 7845 5000
Fax: +44 20 7845 5055
Email: sales@thameshudson.co.uk
www.thamesandhudson.com

For distribution in the USA and Canada please contact:
English Language Support Office
AVA Publishing (UK) Ltd.
Tel: +44 1903 204 455
Email: enquiries@avabooks.co.uk

ISBN 2-940373-07-8

10 9 8 7 6 5 4 3 2 1

Design by studio 7.5, Berlin
English translation by Victor Dewsbery, Berlin

Production and separations by AVA Book Production Pte. Ltd., Singapore
Tel: +65 6334 8173
Fax: +65 6334 0752
Email: production@avabooks.com.sg

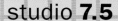

studio **7.5**

Designing for

Small Screens

Mobile Phones I Smart Phones

PDAs I Pocket PCs

Navigation Systems

MP3 Players

Game Consoles

Chapter 1   014|027

Small is Beautiful

Visual Timeline: The Implementation of Miniaturisation **014**

Chapter 2   028|047

The Screen

Particularities of Small Screens **030**
Techniques to Increase the Screen Surface Area **030**
How to Divide the Screen **037**

Chapter 3   048|073

Physical Interaction

Physical Interaction **050**
Interaction Techniques and Elements **052**
Instant Feedback **060**
Natural Mapping: The Position of Control Elements **061**
Natural Mapping: The Movement of the Control Elements **062**
Motor Memory **063**

Chapter 4   074|093

Large Structures on Small Screens

The Mental Model **076**
Context **078**
Analogue and Digital **079**
Organising Information **080**
Location **082**
Alphabetical Order **084**
Time Sequence **084**
Category **085**
Hierarchy **085**
Shallow Hierarchies **086**
Steep Hierarchies **087**

B

Moore's
Glossar
Battery

Scaling Down Websites and Applications **038**
Dynamic Organisation of Space **040**

Screen
Glossar
Screen
Display

User-friendly Soft Key Designs **064**
Text Input Solutions **066**
Innovative Interaction Concepts **068**
Alternative Forms of Physical Interaction **070**

Touchsc
The Ess

Calendar and Diary Functionality **088**
Visualising Spatial Information **090**

Commu

Chapter 5 094|105

The Network on Small Screens

Metaphors **096**
Databases **096**
Different Output Media **098**

Chapter 6 106|115

Entertainment on Small Screens

Entertainment Value **108**
Games **108**
The Logic of Games **108**
Moving Image **109**
Sound **109**

Chapter 7 116|137

Digital Hieroglyphs:
Text and Icons on Small Screens

Text **118**
Icons **124**

Chapter 8 138|155

Layout and Colour on
Small Screens

Visual Perception and the Small Screen **138**
Colour on Small Screens **144**

Chapter 9 156|169

Developing Designs for
Small Screens

The Scenario **158**
The Paper Computer **158**
The Organisational Diagram **159**
Simulation **159**
Evaluation **159**

A

Sources 170|171
Index 172|175

Mobile Information and Entertainment Applications **100**
Networking Small-screen Devices **101**
Creating New Mobile Service Ideas **102**

Glossary of Related Terms **104**
The Generations of Mobile Communications **105**

Creative Editing on Small Screens **110**
The Development of Games and Gaming Techniques **112**

Gaming Classification Systems **114**

Ergonomic Text Display **128**
Designing Effective Icon Alphabets **130**
Image Based Communication Techniques **132**

Screen Fonts **134**
Antialiasing **135**
ClearType Technology **136**
Finetuning Icons for the Screen **136**
Glossary of Related Terms **137**

Highlighting Methods **148**
Colour for Guidance and Coding **150**
Talby Mobile Phone Exemplar **152**

Additive Colour Mixing **154**
Colour Depths **154**
The Essentials of Human Colour Perception **155**

The Paper Computer and other Simulation Techniques **160**
Marwell Zoo Exemplar **162**
Audi AG Exemplar **164**

Development Tools **168**
Webography **169**

B

C

How to get the most out of this book

Not all design concepts that are valid on larger screens can be successfully implemented on smaller ones. A multitude of devices, with very dissimilar technical specifications, fall under the category of those with 'small-screen interfaces', and all these devices differ in size and in their type of display, mode of user interaction and level of performance.

To simplify the complex issues surrounding small-screen interface design, so that they can be visualised and utilised easily, we have structured the book into nine chapters. Each one serves as a complete entity, which allows you to 'dip' in and out of the book's content if you wish to do so. Each of these chapters is then broken down into three sections.

47 mm x 87 mm

To judge the **physical size** of a screen design, the actual size is shown as a wireframe on the page.

Section A

Nowadays smaller screens can display an increasing number of colours. Originally only black and white was available; this progressed to greyscale, and then colour screens. The first colour displays only had a limited range of 16 colours, but nowadays 18 bit screens with more than 200,000 colour shades are available. It is likely that true colour, with its colour depth capacity of 24 bit or 32 bit, will soon be available for use on small-screen devices, thus providing designers the same colour capabilities that they have on larger screens.

When selecting colours for the digital medium, the **intrinsic brightness** of colours in the RGB colour scale must be taken into account – these are different from the brightness effect of CMYK colours.

This difference cannot be shown adequately in print, so the shift in contrast is demonstrated here with a brightness scale.

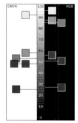

Colour on small screens
Some of the first colour screens used very strong colours; the possibility of using colour led to much exaggeration and a number of almost overpowering initial designs. The fact that small-screen devices are used for shorter periods and with less user concentration than their full-sized counterparts means that the designer must primarily use colour as a means to make the operation of the device as simple as possible. Therefore, colour should be used to direct the user's focus so that they can quickly distinguish what is important and what is unimportant and so be swifter to make their interaction decisions.

The effect of colour **contrast and brightness** also plays an important role on small-screen interfaces. To understand the interaction concept, the screen must be easy to read, even under adverse conditions. An important consideration for legibility on both large and small screens is the contrast in brightness.

Colour is displayed on the screen by mixing the three primary colours of red, green and blue in an additive mixture. Colours generated by additive colour mixing are characterised by the fact that their resulting secondary colours will be significantly brighter than the primary colours because extra light will have been transmitted. This will serve to exaggerate or distort the intrinsic brightness of colour families, and affects the contrasts between different colours and combinations of colour on the screen. An absolute brightness contrast of 50% should be exceeded for all important content on the screen.

The **absolute brightness contrast** should always be more than 50%; if necessary this value should be checked by converting the colours to a greyscale.

Brightness and contrast can be used systematically to enhance the the depth of the screen. This means that content that is in the background or is currently inactive should appear darker in colour and with lower contrast and colour saturation. Content that is curr windows or pop-
contrast and colour saturation. These principles support figure/ground perception and also help the user to grasp the structure and interaction of the system quickly.

Spatial impact can be further enhanced by a systematic selection of the colour family. Cold colours can be used to visually form the background, whereas warmer colours tend to appear in the foreground and closer to the user.

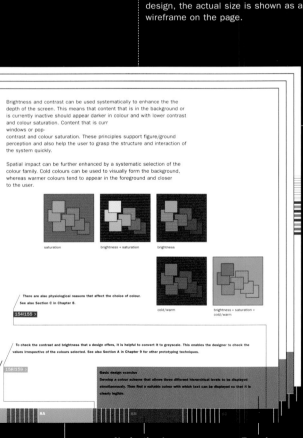

saturation   brightness + saturation   brightness

cold/warm   brightness + saturation + cold/warm

There are also physiological reasons that affect the choice of colour. See also Section C in Chapter 8.

154|155 >

To check the contrast and brightness that a design offers, it is helpful to convert it to greyscale. This enables the designer to check the values irrespective of the colours selected. See also Section A in Chapter 9 for other prototyping techniques.

158|159 >

Basic design exercise
Develop a colour scheme that allows three different hierarchical levels to be displayed simultaneously. Then find a suitable colour with which text can be displayed so that it is clearly legible.

144|145 Layout and Colour on Small Screens

8A   9B   9C

Link   **Navigation bar**   **Exercise**

The **first section** of each chapter is dedicated to a theoretical reflection of the issue in question, and provides an overview of the various design options that relate to this issue.

The **second section** of each chapter offers examples of good practice and shows how the theory of the first section can be practically applied.

The **third section** of each chapter offers supplementary information, such as the technological basics that will help you to make informed design decisions. This information is accompanied by statistics on user behaviour and glossaries that decodes technical jargon, terminology and acronyms. For better understanding and where applicable individual glossary entries can be found in order of logical succession, otherwise the entries appear in alphabetical order

To aid **navigation through this book**, each of the three sections is colour-coded. Wherever useful tips, hints, complementary or further information can be found, we have listed cross-references to other chapters or sections of the book. A navigation bar positioned at the bottom of the page eases access to the chapters and sections, and helps you to locate linked information.

The individual chapters also contain **questions** and **assignments** that challenge you to be creative and develop conceptual or formal designs for small screens.

Section B

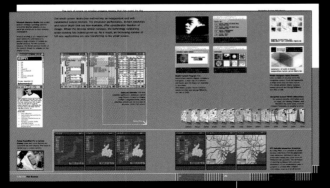

Section C

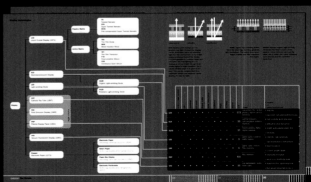

Introduction

Since the invention of the transistor, miniaturisation has been the main phenomenon that has distinguished electronics from all other areas of technology. We have grown used to the fact that computers and computerised devices have become ever smaller and increasingly powerful. Portable laptop computers could soon replace desktop PCs as the computers that are used for most applications.

Nowadays, there is an increasing number of devices that are even smaller than laptops. In fact, they are as small as current technology allows, and as big as the respective application requires. For example, if we are to be accessible by telephone at all times, then clearly the telephone must be small enough for us to take it with us wherever we go. The same applies to electronic address books, jotting pads, digital cameras or combined devices that include all of these functions. All of these devices are specialised computers to a greater or lesser extent. When we speak of 'personal' computers we immediately think of a monitor, a keyboard and a mouse, but we will soon have to change our way of thinking. It is so much more 'personal' to have a device that never leaves our side because it is so small, light and portable. Even though computers in mobile-phone format still raise a smile in comparison with the muscle power (expressed in gigabytes and gigahertz), of their static competition, the advantages of a 'really' personal computer are nevertheless obvious.

Just as the concept of the personal computer was dismissed in the late 1970s as a fancy gadget, contemporary devices are still underestimated today – simply because they are small.

Whether this new revolution of small devices will be successful depends largely on whether the interface can shrink to keep pace with the hardware. At present, the miniaturisation of computer hardware stands in stark contrast to the development of the computer software. Bigger and bigger monitors, with an ever higher resolution, have tempted developers to be increasingly wasteful of screen space in applications on standard personal computers.

The strategies of software design can only be transferred from the 'big' devices to their 'small' counterparts to a very limited extent. This means that the development of the user interface is the crucial factor in the design process, just as it was in the development of the first generation of personal computers. That is why we believe that this book is necessary – to equip young designers with concepts to help them face this challenge.

Chapter 1

Small is Beautiful

In these two combined sections we have created a visual timeline that charts the development of technological devices, both portable and desktop. As technology has evolved so too has the implementation of miniaturisation and the sophistication of functionality.

A+B

In this section we explain the relationship between time and technological advancement, in accordance with Moore's Law. This is coupled with a short glossary of terms and a detailed explanation of battery types.

C

The small, portable devices of today would not be possible without some of the inventions and advances of the last 130 years. The roots of this development lie in communication media and devices such as the telephone and radio, and in the inventions of information technology, for example, transistors and personal computers. The miniaturisation of hardware, in combination with digital and wireless transmission technology allows mobile and personal devices, which can accompany us at all times.

1876: sees the **birth of the telephone**. The first historical words spoken by Alexander Graham Bell on the night of the 10th March are: "Mr. Watson, come here; I want you!"

1936: the **Zuse Z1** is the first program-controlled binary computer. It is mainly relay based and can perform eight different commands: read numbers from memory, write numbers to memory, decimal-binary conversion, binary-decimal conversion, addition, subtraction, multiplication and division.

1938: Canadian Al Gross, invents the **walkie-talkie**. Eleven years later he also patents the telephone pager, which did not become a great success until the 1970s.

1946: John von Neumann creates a **Computing Machine** that uses a single-storage structure to hold both the set of instructions on how to perform the computation and the data required or generated by the computation. Most modern computers still use this architecture.

1894: Italian Guglielmo Marconi invents the **radio**.

1928: in London, John Logie Baird performs the world's first **colour image transmission**.

1946: AT&T Corporation launches the first commercial **mobile telephone service** for private customers.

1921: the combination of the **telephone and radio** enables officers at the Detroit Michigan Police Department to communicate with each other from patrol car to patrol car.

1947: William Shockley invents the 'transfer resistance device', later known as the **transistor**. It revolutionises the incorporated electronics and gives the transistor a reliability that could not be achieved with vacuum tubes.

1927: **the first transatlantic phone call**

1935: **the first phone call around the world**

1875   1880   1885   1890   1895   1900   1905   1910   1915   1920   1925   1930   1935   1940   1945   1950   1955

1968: Douglas Engelbart invents an 'X-Y Position Indicator' to assist user navigation on a computer screen. Twenty years later, as the **computer mouse**, it becomes the standard input device for personal computers.

1968: Alan Kay's **Dynabook** is heralded as a vision of a portable computer that everybody can use. It is to be so simple that even a child could operate the device.
The technology to implement such a product does not yet exist, but the Dynabook is the forerunner of the laptop and PDA. Other contributions by Alan Kay and his team at Xerox PARC include the graphical user interface, the laser printer, the client server network model, Ethernet and object-oriented programming.

1973: Sharp releases the **EL-805 LCD calculator**, starting a revolution in electronics. Until now, calculators used fluorescent character display tubes or light-emitting diodes. Using LCD for the number display means that the power consumption is cut dramatically to a mere 1% of the consumption of previous calculators. This astonishing leap in energy efficiency provides 100 hours of use from a single AA battery.

1963: Bell Labs introduce the **touch-tone telephone** to replace rotary dial telephones. This paves the way for telephone services such as short text messaging.

1963: Ivan Edward Sutherland invents the **Sketchpad**, which makes it possible to create graphic images directly on to a display screen via the use of a hand-held object such as a light pen.

1971: American scientist James Fergason discovers the 'twisted-nematic' **LCD**. He produces the first practical displays in 1969 and submits an application for the patent in 1971. One of the first customers is the Gruen watchmaking company.

1972: Motorola presents the design for its **portable radio telephone 'DynaTAC'** (Dynamic Adaptive Total Area Coverage). This prototype of the world's first commercial portable telephone uses cellular radio technology. Dr. Martin Cooper, a former general manager of the systems division at Motorola, is considered to be the inventor of the first portable handset and the first person to make a call on a portable cell phone in April 1973. The first call he makes is to his rival, Joel Engel, who is the head of research at Bell Labs.

1962: Telstar is the first **active communications satellite** in space.

1969: sees the birth of the internet. The 'Defense Advanced Research Projects Agency' (DARPA) begins the **DARPA internet programme**.

1971: the computer engineer Ray Tomlinson invents internet-based **electronic mail**, making it possible to send messages to another person over a network. The first e-mail message sent is 'QWERTYUIOP'.

1976: the **Apple Computer** company is created in a Californian garage by school friends Steven Wozniak and Steve Jobs.

1973: researchers at the the Xerox Palo Alto Research Center develop the Xerox Alto, the first PC prototype with a **graphical user interface**. But this user-friendly system with icons, menus, cascading windows and dialogue boxes will only be commercially marketed in 1981 with the **Xerox Star**. Its 17-inch screen has 1024 x 800 pixels.

1981: Adam Osborne develops the **first portable computer**. The Osborne I weighs 24 pounds, costs $1,795 and features 64 kilobytes of memory. Its 5-inch screen has 52 x 24 pixels.

1977: the **Commodore PET 2001** enters the market in the USA and is an immediate success. It is a computer developed for the private sphere rather than for commercial use. 'PET' is an acronym for 'Personal Electronic Transactor'. Its 9-inch screen has 320 x 200 pixels.

1980: sees the introduction of the world's smallest and cheapest computer – the **Sinclair ZX80**. It measures 9 x 7 inches and costs £99.95. In order to keep the price so low the designers had to introduce some radical ideas to reduce the number of components. The biggest saving is the use of a domestic television set as a monitor and a cassette player as a program and data-storage device.

1981: IBM brings the **personal computer** on to the market. Its hardware architecture becomes the industry standard and the abbreviation 'PC' is a recognised term for desktop computers. Its operating system MS-DOS is the foundation stone on which Bill Gates will build his Microsoft empire. This PC has a four-colour screen and a resolution of 320 x 200 pixels.

1980: Nintendo's Game & Watch console, Ball, is the world's first commercially successful **mobile LCD screen game**.

1984: the **Apple Macintosh** begins its victorious march around the world and launches the concept of desktop publishing. Its 9-inch screen has 512 x 342 pixels.

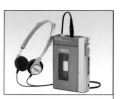

1979: sees the introduction of the TPS-L2 **Sony Walkman.** The first portable audio-cassette player.

1982: Nintendo brings out the first portable Game & Watch console with **two screens** of 5.3 x 3.5 mm each.

1984: the **Psion 1** is recognised as the first **PDA** (Personal Digital Assistant). It features a clock, a calendar, an address book and a calculator.

1982: the first **digital phone exchange** in Europe

1978: the first **1G** telephone system is launched in America

1985: sees the first **portable phone.** This device incorporated a handset, an antenna and a power pack and is designed to be carried on a shoulder. The Japanese 'Shoulder Phone 100 type' weighs approximately three kilograms.

1994: **Magic Cap** (Communicating Applications Platform), is designed for ease of use and intuitive communication. Disarmingly simple and sublimely powerful, it is designed and built by a team of engineers led by the co-founders of General Magic: Bill Atkinson and Andy Hertzfeld, and it forms the interface for a new breed of personal communicators such as the **Sony Magic Link**. Its 5.4-inch screen has 480x320 pixels.

1989: the **Macintosh Portable** is Apple's first attempt at launching a 'laptop'. It is received with critical acclaim, but has very poor sales in the marketplace. It features a black and white active-matrix LCD screen that is incorporated into a hinged lid, and this lid covers the keyboard when the machine is not in use. Instead of a mouse it has an integrated trackball, which is positioned to the right of the keyboard. Expensive SRAM memory is used to maximise battery life. Its 9.8-inch screen has 640x400 pixels.

1989: the **Game Boy** is introduced as an 8-bit hand-held console with a green monochrome screen that has four brightness levels. Today the Game Boy is in its third generation and Nintendo claims that the Game Boy is the most successful video game system of all time. Its 2.5-inch screen has 160x144 pixels.

1994: the **first satellite call** is made using the Nokia 2140.

1993: Apple presents its **Newton MessagePad 100** It is the first PDA with true handwriting recognition. Its 5.5-inch screen has 240x320 pixels.

1989: the first of 24 satellites that form the current **GPS** constellation (Block II), is put into orbit on 14 February. The initial tests with Block I satellites began in 1978.

1992: the **first mobile phone for digital networks** comes to Europe. The Motorola International 3200 has a distinctive 'bone' shape, measures 334x43x67mm and weighs half a kilogram.

1993: the first **2G** telephone service is launched by Nokia. 2G phones use GSM for voice services and allow relatively **low-speed** data services to be used for text messaging and WAP internet access.

1987: the first **SMS** service is launched in Japan.

9.6 Kbps

1985

1990

1995

1A

1B

1C

1996: Jeff Hawkins, who then headed
Palm Computing, carves a block of wood
into an object that he could comfortably
fit into his hand, and he carries it in his
shirt pocket for several weeks.
Eventually, he shapes and refines the
design and the **Palm Pilot** is born.
The Palm Pilot's 4-inch screen has a
resolution of 160x160 pixels.

1996: **Tamagotchi**, the digital pet, makes
its mark in popular-cultural history when
Bandai launches the product in 1996. It
sells more than 40 million units worldwide.

1997: the Nokia 6110 is the first mobile
phone to come with **built-in electronic games**.
Nokia first introduces the snake game; since
then the number and variety of games
available has grown dramatically.

1998: the **Game Boy Color** is introduced
by Nintendo as the first game console with
a colour display. In principle the device
can display 32,000 colours, but it can
display only 56 colours simultaneously.
The 2.3-inch screen has 160x140 pixels.

1996: sees the launch of the first
'Smart Phone'. The Nokia 9000
Communicator is not just a mobile
phone, it also offers Internet access
and the ability to send and receive
e-mails, faxes and SMS messages.
Its screen has 640x200 pixels.

1997: **MP3.com** is created by Michael
Robertson as an internet platform for the
distribution of digital music.

1997: the Siemens S10 is the first **mobile
phone with a 'colour' display**. It is just
about possible to recognise four colours on
its 97x54 pixel screen.

1999: NTT DoCoMo launches
i-mode in Japan.

1996   1997   1998   1999

2000: Ericsson unveils its T36; the first **Bluetooth mobile phone**. The built-in Bluetooth chip makes wireless connectivity possible between the phone and other mobile devices.

2001: the debut of the **iPod**. The first generation iPod can store up to 10,000 songs, and has a liquid-crystal display with LED backlighting, which allows the artist's name, song and album title to be displayed. The iPod's 2-inch screen has 160 x 128 pixels.

2000: the first **mobile phone with a colour display** is introduced to the Japanese market. The Mitsubishi D502iHYPER can display 256 colours and its screen has 96 x 120 pixels.

2000: Sharp releases the first **camera phone**. The J-SH04 features an integrated 110,000-pixel CMOS image sensor for digital photography, and its screen has 96 x 130 pixels.

The FOMA phones, such as the NEC N2001, are the first devices with an OLED display and their 2.2-inch screens have 120 x 160 pixels. Unlike TFT displays, these displays are not backlit, so the screen can be kept slim. However, there are problems with the durability of the devices, so **OLED displays** disappear from the market until 2004.

2000: Samsung Electronics develops the world's **first TV phone** SCH-M220. The user can watch TV on the 1.8-inch TFT display for up to 200 minutes on a single battery charge.

2000: LG Information and Communications introduces the world's first mobile phone with an integrated MP3 internet music player that uses a **flash memory card**. The device, the CyON MP3 LG-P810, has a stamp-sized SanDisk 16 MB or 32 MB multimedia card.

2000: **2.5G** is a modification of 2G, adding packet data transmission that increases data **transmission speeds**.

2001: NTT DoCoMo becomes the first mobile phone provider in the world to offer **3G** mobile phone services under the acronym 'FOMA' (Freedom Of Mobile Multimedia Access). 3G phones use UMTS or CDMA 2000 technology and therefore offer **high-speed internet access**.

48–144 Kbps

144 Kbps–2+ Mbps

2000

2001

2002: the **first ring tone service**, CHAKU-UTA, enters the market. It enables users to download songs in their original format and use these songs as the dial tones on mobile phones.

2002: the Sharp SH251iS is the world's first mobile phone to incorporate a **3D colour LCD** and **3D editing function**, which enables users to convert 2D images into 3D images.
Its 2.2-inch screen has 176x220 pixels, and can display 65,536 colours.

2002: Sharp introduces the Zaurus SL-C700. The world's first PDA to come equipped with a LCD screen that is capable of outputting **VGA resolution**. Its 3.7-inch screen has 640x480 pixels.

In 2002, the **number of mobile phone subscribers** in the world exceeds the number of landline subscribers for the first time.

2003: sees the launch of the Nokia **N-Gage**. It is the first mobile phone with enough gaming power to compete with Nintendo's Game Boy Advance SP, in terms of program complexity and image quality. The N-Gage's 2.8-inch screen has 176x208 pixels and is capable of displaying 4,096 colours.

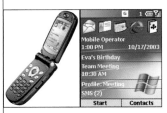

2003: the Motorola MPx200 is the first **mobile phone with a Windows interface**. It offers full MS Office compatibility with the PC and a slot for SD memory cards, which offer up to 1 GB of storage space. Its screen has 176x220 pixels.

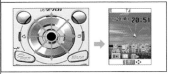

2003: the mobile phone manufacturer NEC brings out the FOMA N2051: the first **mobile phone with a cursor**. The technology that enables this is called 'neuropointer'. The phone's 2.2-inch screen has 176x240 pixels.

2004: the SONY Clie VZ-90 is launched. It is the first **PDA to offer an OLED screen**, producing brilliant, neon-sharp colours that could not be rivalled by LCDs. Its 3.8-inch screen has 480x320 pixels.

2004: anti-virus software developers claim they have discovered the first computer virus that is capable of infecting mobile phones. The **'Cabir Worm'** infects mobile phones running the Symbian operating system and spreads via Bluetooth, which has a range of about 30 meters. It scans for other mobile phones, then sends a copy of itself to the first vulnerable one it finds. The constant scanning leads to a vastly shortened battery life. If the virus succeeds in penetrating the mobile phone, it writes the word 'cabir' on the screen and the virus is then activated every time the phone is turned on.

2004: Sony launches the LIBRIé; the first consumer device to use **e-paper** technology. Its 6-inch screen has a resolution of 170 dpi and 800x600 pixels.

2004: Samsung announces the world's first camera phone with **5-megapixel** resolution. The SCH-S250 also includes the first QVGA display in a mobile phone that supports **16.7 million colours**.
Its 2-inch screen has 240x320 pixels.

2004: in Japan, Vodafone releases the first mobile phone that is capable of receiving **analogue terrestrial television broadcasts**. The NEC V601N has headphones containing a built-in television antenna, and the user can watch TV for about one hour before recharging the battery.

2004: SAMSUNG Electronics unveils the first **mobile phone with a hard drive** – the V5400. A tiny 1.5 GB hard drive in the phone greatly expands the memory capacity. The 2.2-inch screen has 240×320 pixels.

2004: Nintendo launches a new hand-held video-game platform in Japan: the **Nintendo DS**. It has two 3-inch TFT displays, each with a resolution of 256×192 pixels, the ability to display up to 260,000 colours, a touchscreen, voice recognition and two types of wireless network connection.

2004: Sony enters the hand-held video-game market with the launch of its **Playstation Portable** in Japan. The device has a 4.3-inch, 16:9 widescreen TFT display that can display 480×272 pixels and 16.7 million colours. The PSP can be connected to the internet, mobile phones, PCs and other PSPs via WLAN, IrDA and USB.

2005: IBM, Sony and Toshiba present the jointly developed microprocessor **Cell**, which can reach speeds of over 4 GHz. It is first used in the PlayStation 3, and later used to increase the performance of computers, mobile phones and PDAs.

2005: **DMB** (Digital Multimedia Broadcasting) launches in Korea. It is the first service in the world for **digital television on mobile phones**.

2005: Sharp's new model V603SH arrives with a **motion control sensor** that recognises movements and responds to them. This allows customers to perform menu operations or play games by moving the handset up, down, left or right. Its 2.4-inch screen has 320×240 pixels.

2005: the **3.5G** HSDPA is an enhanced version of UMTS technology that increases data **transmission speeds**.

2006: the first DDR (Double Data Rate) chip will come on the market. It will have four times the **storage capacity** of conventional chips. With the development of the prototype DDR3 DRAM (Dynamic Random Access Memory), the Korean technological company Samsung is setting a new standard for the coming generation of ultra-fast, low-power memory chips.

2006: the DMFC (Direct Methanol Fuel Cell) will be launched. The **fuel cell** can supply mobile devices with energy for much longer than conventional lithium-ion batteries. For example, ten hours of battery life is planned for notebooks.

2006: **4G** WWAN networks are expected to be available in Japan in 2006. They will have far higher **data speeds**, which are suitable for high-resolution video and television.

8 Mbps – 20 Mbps

20 Mbps – 300 Mbps

The evolution of small-screen devices would be inconceivable without the **miniaturisation of technology**. The concept that less might mean more for the user was successfully executed by Sony with the launch and subsequent development of their Walkman. The constant reduction of the size and price of technical components creates mobility and the opportunity to achieve ever greater personalisation.

Moore's Law observes that the number of transistors per area doubles every 18 months.

Gordon E. Moore, one of the founders of Intel, observed in 1965 that the number of transistors on a chip almost doubled every year. At the time he assumed that this trend would continue for at least another ten years. However, Moore later increased the period in which the number of transistors doubled to 18 months. This law is still valid today and its logic helps us to understand the reason why technical devices are constantly becoming smaller, cheaper and more efficient.

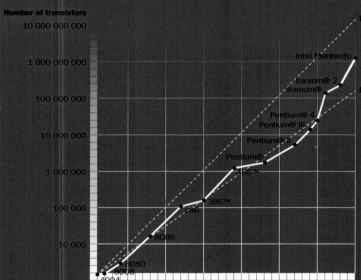

Number of transistors

Doubled every 18 months

Doubled every 24 months

Intel Montecito
Itanium® 2
Itanium®
Pentium® 4
Pentium® III
Pentium® II
Pentium®
486™
386™
286
8086
8080
8008
4004

10 000 000 000
1 000 000 000
100 000 000
10 000 000
1 000 000
100 000
10 000

1970   1975   1980   1985   1990   1995   2000   2005

Source: www.intel.com/research/silicon/mooreslaw.htm

In 2000 the number of **mobile phone connections** in Japan overtook the number of landline connections. Worldwide, it took another two years before there were more mobile phone subscribers than landline subscribers.

Source: Ministry of Public Management, Home Affairs, Posts and Telecommunications, Japan

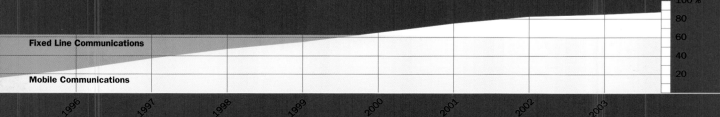

Fixed Line Communications

Mobile Communications

100 %
80
60
40
20

1996   1997   1998   1999   2000   2001   2002   2003

PDA: a Personal Digital Assistant is a small mobile device that has address and calendar management functions as standard. The range of functions available has constantly increased, and most PDAs today also offer internet access and the ability to compose, send and receive e-mails. Entries are made via a mini-keyboard or by stylus and touchscreen, often combined with automatic handwriting recognition.

Pocket PC: this device is similar to a PDA in size and functionality. Its operating system, Windows Mobile from Microsoft, is closely based on the Windows operating system for PCs, thus simplifying the handling and the transfer of data.

Communicator: this is a term that is used to describe a combination of a mobile phone and PDA. It originates from the launch of the Nokia 9000 Communicator, which was the first device of this kind. Nowadays the term 'smart phone' is a more commonly used name for the device.

Japan quickly adopts new advances in technology. The spread of mobile communication technology in Japan in the last few years demonstrates how small **mobile devices** have developed to quickly become natural companions in everyday life.

Source: Ministry of Public Management, Home Affairs, Posts and Telecommunications, Japan

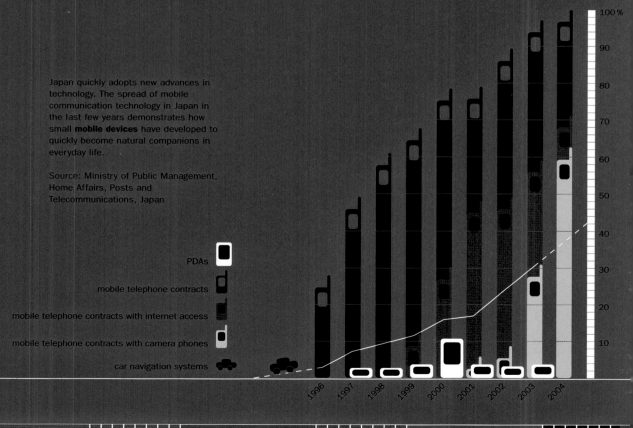

PDAs

mobile telephone contracts

mobile telephone contracts with internet access

mobile telephone contracts with camera phones

car navigation systems

1996 1997 1998 1999 2000 2001 2002 2003 2004

100 %
90
80
70
60
50
40
30
20
10

Nickel Cadmium (NiCd) batteries: the first notebook computers benefited from the advantages of this rechargeable battery technology, which was already in commercial use from 1948 onwards. NiCd batteries quickly provide large amounts of energy for power-hungry components such as the central processing unit (CPU) display or hard drive. The batteries have a long-service life and are moderately priced.

However, cadmium is a toxic heavy metal, and as such requires careful disposal. Another disadvantage is their low specific energy of 40–60 Wh/kg, as well as the **'memory effect'**. This is a permanent reduction of the charging performance if the battery is not always completely emptied. Due to the high charging capacity of NiCd batteries, they are mainly used in devices with a high-power requirement, such as rechargeable power tools, although they are also often used in cordless phones and camcorders because of their low production costs.

Nickel Metal Hydride (NiMH) batteries were developed at the beginning of the 1990s to meet the growing demand for mobile devices. These batteries provide high and constant levels of power for a long time. NiMH batteries are similar in structure to nickel-cadmium batteries, but their specific energy is higher at 60–80 Wh/kg. The disposal of these batteries is less of a problem because they do not contain toxic heavy metals. A significant disadvantage of NiMH batteries is the **'lazy-battery effect'** this temporary reduction of capacity can be inconvenient, but it can be remedied by completely discharging the battery several times.

Due to their good environmental compatibility and high capacity levels, NiMH batteries are mainly used in mobile phones, camcorders, notebooks and audio devices.

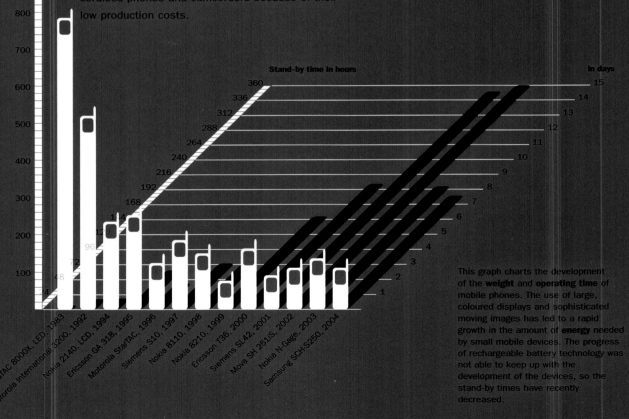

This graph charts the development of the **weight** and **operating time** of mobile phones. The use of large, coloured displays and sophisticated moving images has led to a rapid growth in the amount of **energy** needed by small mobile devices. The progress of rechargeable battery technology was not able to keep up with the development of the devices, so the stand-by times have recently decreased.

Lithium-Ion (Li-ion) batteries were developed at the beginning of the 1990s. They have the highest specific energy of rechargeable systems, at 90–110 Wh/kg, as well as a low self-discharge rate and a long storage time. However, lithium, is used as an electrolyte, which is a highly reactive light metal, and as such it is an easily flammable material that can explode if heated. To ensure safety, lithium-ion batteries have a pressure-relief valve and a pressure-resistant housing, but these necessary safety features are reflected in the price. A rechargeable Li-ion battery is approximately 30 percent more expensive than a NiMH battery. Lithium-ion technology has a higher energy storage than conventional batteries such as NiCd and NiMH, but the batteries do not reach the same capacity. Lithium-ion batteries are mainly used in mobile phones and notebooks.

Lithium-polymer (Li-polymer) batteries adopt the same working principle as lithium-ion batteries, but with the exception that the electrolytes are in gel rather than liquid form; so these batteries will not leak. Li-polymer batteries are not forced to adopt the classical cylindrical or rectangular shapes of other batteries because they are composed of aluminium or metalised plastic foil, which can be moulded into almost any shape. As such, any hollow spaces in battery-operated devices can easily be filled with a bespoke li-polymer battery.

Zinc-air batteries: the development of zinc-air batteries is still in its infancy, but the technology behind them is not new. All of the components used in zinc-air batteries are free from any harmful toxic substances and are easy to recycle. Zinc-air technology is therefore environmentally-friendly and inexpensive. Further advantages of these batteries are their high capacity and their low self-discharge rate when sealed (air-tight). Due to its high specific energy capacity of up to 350 Wh/kg, zinc-air technology is used mainly in hearing aids and personal alarm devices. The first prototypes for use in portable devices are still in the development phase.

Direct Methanol Fuel Cell (DMFC) has the greatest potential for the future as fuel-cell technology has greater efficiency and energy density than any present battery systems. In recent years, companies such as Motorola, NEC, Samsung, Fujitsu, Hitachi, Casio and Toshiba have presented prototypes of direct methanol fuel cells. The manufacturers plan to market the first commercially usable cells during 2006.

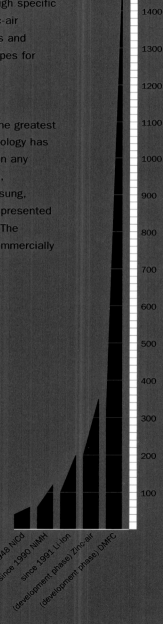

Specific energy in Wh/kg

Comparison of the different rechargeable battery systems and their specific energy values.

since 1948 NiCd
since 1990 NiMH
since 1991 Li-Ion
(development phase) Zinc-air
(development phase) DMFC

Chapter 2

In this chapter we look at the specification particularities of small screens and what distinguishes them from their larger relatives. Techniques that help to virtually increase the screen size, and thus compensate for the limited surface area, are also explained. From dialogue boxes and menus, to panning and disproportional zoom, all contemporary design concepts of screen-space management are introduced.

A

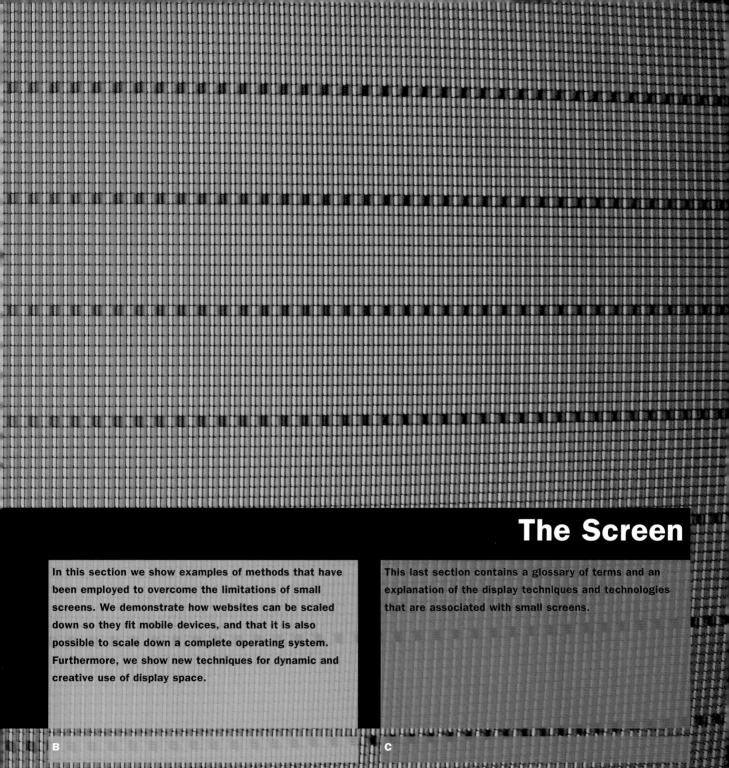

The Screen

In this section we show examples of methods that have been employed to overcome the limitations of small screens. We demonstrate how websites can be scaled down so they fit mobile devices, and that it is also possible to scale down a complete operating system. Furthermore, we show new techniques for dynamic and creative use of display space.

B

This last section contains a glossary of terms and an explanation of the display techniques and technologies that are associated with small screens.

C

The screen is the primary interface of any digitised medium, it interacts with the most powerful of the human senses: sight. As such it constitutes the most powerful form of interaction between man and machine. The screen's high performance is derived from the fact that it allows synchronous optical perception – the user can receive numerous and varied items of information at the same time. It is quite easy to view multiple signals at once, but it is harder or can even be impossible to hear just two signals simultaneously. Thus the rationale behind the development of ever larger screens for desktop computers is quite simply that the larger the display surface, the more information can be rendered simultaneously in a single context.

Particularities of small screens

The small-screen display on portable devices presents the problem of a drastically reduced display area in comparison to the screens of larger devices. In addition, the different uses that have emerged for portable devices must be taken into account; the product and its 'babyface' are not always the sole focus of the user's attention. Increasingly, the use of a small device is only one of several tasks being performed concurrently. Another important difference is that portable devices are often used in a variety of environments and many of these will not always offer an ideal or constant ambient lighting.

Techniques to increase the screen surface area

Since the available screen space of any portable device is almost always smaller than the amount of data to be represented, a number of techniques have emerged to increase the display size by virtual means. These techniques include zooming and panning, as well as the incorporation of windows and dialogue boxes. However, some of these techniques are more suited to small-screen devices than others.

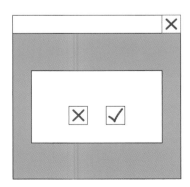

Dialogue boxes are best described as windows that have a fixed size and position, which 'pop-up' in various linear user-guidance situations. Dialogue boxes will take priority over anything in the background, and the message in this window must be accepted by the user before the original application can be resumed. Dialogue boxes are easily transferred to small screens and are often used as interface elements to offer the user clear, step-by-step guidance.

Windows that can be freely moved, enlarged, reduced and closed are not yet used on small screens, as the available space is too small to allow flexible movement. Interaction with windows on a portable device is further complicated because it requires the use of both hands.

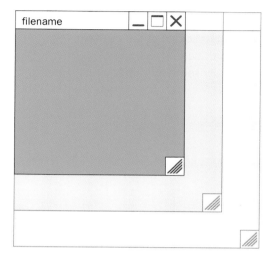

Windows incorporate the following functions:

1. A **title bar** containing the name of the window. This bar also acts as the handle to move the window. This function is not suitable for small-screen devices.

2. An area to **close** the window. This function is also needed on small screens.

3. An optional area to **maximise** the window in order for it to fill the screen.

4. An optional function to **dock** the window at the bottom of the screen. This function can also be transferred to the small screen.

5. A **scale** function, usually in the lower right-hand corner, which is used to enlarge or reduce the window. This function is not suitable for use on smaller screens.

Windows, dialogue boxes, scroll bars, buttons and form fields are generally defined within the operating system itself, so it is not always possible to design them for individual applications. If individually designed interface elements are incorporated into applications, then they should be sufficiently different in appearance to the interface elements supplied by the operating system, but at the same time offer coherent uses. See also Section C in Chapter 4: Large Structures on Small Screens.

Tabs can be regarded as windows that are placed on top of one another, in a similar fashion to an index-card system. This organisational principle is an efficient concept that enables users to call on many options quickly, and the technique can also be used on small-screen displays. The categories shown on the tabs, which always remain visible, help to make the navigation of complex structures manageable. As such, tabs are a good alternative to pull-down and pop-up menus, but there should not be more than five to seven tabs displayed at the same time, otherwise the structure becomes confusing. Double rows of horizontal tabs should be avoided on small screens because they make the relationship between navigation and available space for the content too unfavourable.

The horizontal layout imposes a limit on the amount of text that can be displayed, but this can be overcome by using icons. Tabs offer robust navigation especially for devices operated with one hand via a mini joystick.

Tabs at the top edge of the screen should be avoided if content is to be entered with a stylus, because the content will be covered by the hand holding the stylus.

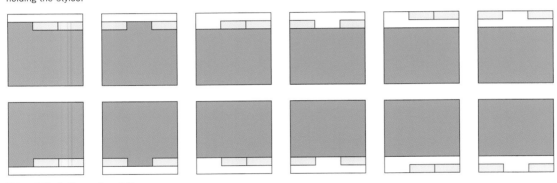

Tabs at the bottom edge of the screen are very suitable for small-screen displays. Used here, there are different ways of organising the navigation area and separating it from the content.

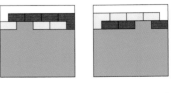

Multi-row tabs should always be avoided because the position of individual categories keeps changing, which can lead to confusion. On small screens they take up too much space in relation to the content that is presented.

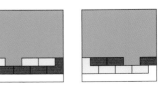

Pull-down and pop-up menus offer a selection of options that are presented in list form. A pull-down menu drops down from the top edge of the screen, whereas a pop-up menu opens up from the bottom edge of the screen. Pull-down menus will be familiar as they are frequently used for the quick selection of fields in forms. Pull-down and pop-up menus have become established in many applications on small screens, as they can be used instead of entering text in order to confirm a selection. Both types of menu are often used on pocket PCs, this is because, ideally, applications on small screens will be instantly recognisable to the user by offering an environment on the small screen that resembles that of its large-screen counterparts.

However, there are still design considerations to be taken into account: pop-up menus are a better choice for devices where a stylus is used for the interaction because, unlike pull-down menus, the items are not covered by your hand. Pop-up menus on mobile phones cover most of the screen, so their interaction priority resembles that of a dialogue box.

Pull-down menus are useful on small screens if they are used in ways that comply with the expectations of the user. For example, this pull-down menu could apply to the small-screen versions of desktop applications.

Nested pull-down menus should be avoided on small screens if there is a risk that they could be wider, or longer, than the available screen space when expanded.

Pop-up menus are a better alternative to pull-down menus on stylus-based devices and are often used as context menus.

Nested pop-up menus employ similar principles to those of nested pull-down menus. If it is necessary to create extra sub-menus, care must be taken to ensure that the element does not expand beyond the limits of the screen. If the sub-menu relates to a function, a combination of tabs and pop-up menus is advisable.

Basic design exercise

Try to organise all the items that a pizza delivery service might offer in the available space of a hand-held screen. What does it look like if you use a pull-down menu to display the options? Compare it with the potential of a tab solution. Hint: if you are wondering how to visualise your concept, take a look at the different prototyping techniques discussed in Chapter 9.

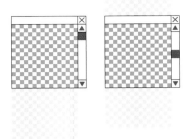

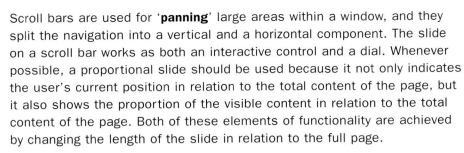

Scroll bars are used for '**panning**' large areas within a window, and they split the navigation into a vertical and a horizontal component. The slide on a scroll bar works as both an interactive control and a dial. Whenever possible, a proportional slide should be used because it not only indicates the user's current position in relation to the total content of the page, but it also shows the proportion of the visible content in relation to the total content of the page. Both of these elements of functionality are achieved by changing the length of the slide in relation to the full page.

Scroll bars on small-screen devices are typically used to navigate the whole screen, and usually in just one direction – vertically (as their main purpose is to navigate through longer text documents, which do not fit on a single screen page). Horizontal scroll bars are rarely used on small screens, simply because there are very few applications that use landscape formats. Vertical navigation also lends itself more easily to the single-handed, thumb-based operations, which many small-screen devices incorporate.

The combination of vertical and horizontal scroll bars should be avoided on small screens. The division of the panning motion into a vertical and a horizontal component makes navigation of large documents clumsy and awkward. A better option is to use a navigation border that runs all around the screen, as this will enable the content to be moved freely in any direction.

Vertical **scroll bars** are placed on the right. In addition to the slide, two arrow buttons are positioned at the top and bottom end of the scroll bar, which can be used for continuous scrolling in either direction.

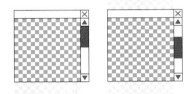

Proportional scroll bars indicate how much of the total content is displayed on the screen or in the window. This information is very useful on small-screen devices, but this feature also has its limitations.

If the total amount of information to be displayed is very large, then proportional scroll bars are not ideal as it is likely that the slide will be too small or its size indication function will be too inaccurate.

The simultaneous use of **vertical and horizontal scroll bars** is awkward and difficult on small screens and should be avoided.

The panning of a screen segment by means of **arrow buttons** placed within a navigation border works well, and it is even better if more buttons can be incorporated to allow the selection of more directions. The navigation border thus offers a continuous array of options for ease of navigation.

If an application incorporates a number pull-down menus, which have long option or item lists, then the menus themselves may require their own scroll bar. This is sometimes essential, but as a rule it should be avoided because it needs a great deal of manual skill from the user, especially if entry is with a stylus, and this is not always possible in all mobile situations. Instead it is better to split the menus, lists and options into several steps so that the user's response or selection can be restricted to limited choices and shorter lists.

On the screens of mobile devices that have a jog dial or joystick, a type of miniature scroll bar has become commonplace. Its physical movement visually supports the navigation of the menu, marking both the length of the list and the current position in the list, but it is only used for display, rather than interaction.

To support '**leafing**', the content of a window or a screen must be split into portions and the user's view will show an indication of the current portion and total number of portions at all times. This information structure, which is borrowed from conventional book printing, is often used on digital applications and it allows the design principles of printed documents to be used on the screen. On larger screens, scrolling is often the appropriate technique to adopt because it would be artificial to interrupt the text flow by portioning the content. However, on small screens, leafing is often a more robust form of text representation.

The mobile use of most small-screen devices makes it more difficult to read the content line by line. Moreover the type of input interaction will determine which method is preferable. If the screen navigation is achieved with a stylus, then scrolling is more complicated than leafing. On a mobile phone, however, scrolling is a one-handed operation and therefore better than leafing. Similarly if the content to be displayed is continuous text, then leafing is a better method, but scrolling is more appropriate for lists.

Leafing offers a traditional way to work in a limited space. The layout of the content can be optimised for the format or size in question. Unlike scrolling, leafing does not produce random views of the content; only controlled portions are accessible. For ease of use, a 'start' and 'end' button should be added as well as the forward and backward functions, and there should be a digital indication of the total number of pages and the current page.

Advanced design exercise

Try to come up with additional functions that a scroll bar can provide the user with.

For example, is there a design solution that will allow a scroll bar to highlight important parts within the text?

Or is there a way to visualise what part of a scrollable page is the most popular?

In **proportional zoom**, the content is
enlarged and therefore an increasing
amount of the content is off the screen.
In some applications, such as in map
navigation, the zoom is combined with
a pan function to make navigation
more flexible.

In **non-proportional zoom**, only parts of
the screen are magnified (instead of an
even magnification of the whole screen).
In those applications where a magnified
part is displayed as an extract that is
laid over the content, this is called a
'magnifying glass' function.

If the content is distorted to enlarge
specific areas, this is called a
disproportional zoom.

In **flip zoom**, the content is broken
into distorted sections and each of
these can be enlarged within the
original context.

Zoom functionality is a technique that allows a large amount of content to
be accessible in a small space, but interaction with 'zoomable' content is
highly demanding – even on large screens. The parameters that the
designer must take into account include the focus of the zoom, the zoom
stages, the plus and minus direction of the zoom and the maximum zoom-
in and zoom-out values. The zoom can act as an automatic partial
magnification of the display, for example with a virtual magnifying glass, or
the user can define all the parameters themselves. Optimum navigation in
free zooming is best when the application allows continuous zooming and
free selection of the focus point, but this requires very extensive
programming and powerful hardware. The quality of zoomable applications
on small screens is still far from ideal, mainly because of the processor
speed of the devices, but even so, zoom offers excellent functionality,
especially in the efficient use of the limited space on small screens.
Zooming can be used to bring together different hierarchical levels in a
plausible way and thus create a logical link between the overview and
detailed content information, so it is a design concept with great potential.

How to divide the screen

Depending on the proportions of the screen, the designer must decide how the available space can be most efficiently subdivided. For vertical formats, a static navigation area should be situated on the short side of the screen: either at the top or bottom. This especially applies to text-based applications, because this structure provides the maximum line length for reading.

Horizontal formats automatically offer more space to arrange the content within a pleasant and legible column width. However, the problem here is that only a few lines of text can be displayed at any one time, and the user will be required to scroll even for short texts. Therefore, a static navigation area on the short side of the screen is again recommended, i.e. either the right or left edge. For devices that require the use of a stylus, the navigation zone should be on the right so that the user's hand does not cover the screen (as most users are more likely to operate their device with the right hand). This restriction does not apply to interaction with a jog dial or joystick.

All concepts that can be used to increase the efficient use of screen space are linked directly to the type of interaction with the screen. So all design decisions must be coordinated with the interaction system of the device. See also Chapter 3: Physical Interaction.

048|049 >

For text applications there is also an additional option available called 'semantic zoom'. See also Chapter 7: Digital Hieroglyphs: Text and Icons on Small Screens.

116|117 >

The small-screen device has evolved into an independent and well-established output medium. The processor performance, screen resolution and colour depth that are now available, offer considerable freedom of design. Whilst the devices remain compact, the technology supporting small-screens has indeed grown-up. As a result, an increasing number of full-size applications are now transferring to the small screen.

Microsoft Windows Mobile: the smaller versions of large operating systems reflect the familiar patterns of use, which are well-known to their desktop counterparts.

Vertical scrolling is the simplest and most commonly used method to present large volumes of content on smaller screens. For this purpose, however, the layout and line breaks of the content should be adapted for the smaller format.

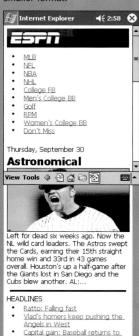

DateLens Calendar: with this calendar application, automatic partial magnification is used to display multiple navigation levels, which provides context and an overview at any time. (240 x 320 pixels)

58 mm x 77 mm

Canon PowerShot Pro 1 Camera Display: more and more devices are controlled via their display. The focus is carried out in a zoom window.

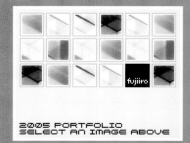

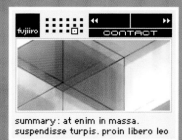

2005 PORTFOLIO
SELECT AN IMAGE ABOVE

Mobile Concert Program: this miniaturised website display contains a tour guide, a video clip of a concert, and music and dial tones are available to download.
(The dream project: Adobe Systems, twenty2product and George Williams, see also p 148)

Mobile Designers Online Portfolio: here, a matrix of 18 dots forms the navigation system. Each dot represents a single work that has been stored. (The dream project: Adobe Systems, twenty2product and George Williams, see also p 148)

Navigation System H9000 (Mitsubishi): for viewing complex information such as maps, the viewing distance, and therefore the zoom level, must be changed frequently on smaller screens.

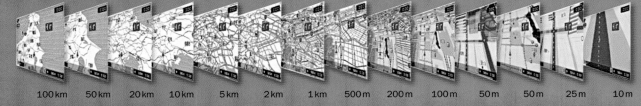

| 100 km | 50 km | 20 km | 10 km | 5 km | 2 km | 1 km | 500 m | 200 m | 100 m | 50 m | 50 m | 25 m | 10 m |

NTT DoCoMo Interactive Streetmap: by using Flash, it is possible to create dynamic interfaces that are graphically more attractive. Information can be processed visually and other forms of interaction are possible. The technique of zooming combined with a strong abstraction of the presentation make it possible to present this complex information, even on a small screen.

2A · 2B · 2C

The lack of space on smaller screens means that the quest for the **dynamic organisation of space** is one of the most challenging aspects associated with the design process.

It is difficult or impossible to view normal websites on a small screen.

Nokia 6630: the individual files here are arranged like a carousel. This permits fast scrolling and the presentation of each file as a thumbnail make it easier to find the content.

The **collapse-to-zoom** concept first offers a thumbnail preview in which the user can select a specific item of interest and display it.

Collapse-to-zoom enables columns within a layout to be temporarily compressed so that other parts of the content have more space. (Visualisation and Interaction Research Group at Microsoft Research: Baudisch, Xie, Wang, and Ma, 2004)

W21S (Sony Ericsson, au by KDDI):
in order to shorten navigation paths
through different menu levels, the first
two levels are tied together as a
crossing. Moving vertically is switching
within the second navigational level
while moving horizontally is switching
within the main menu.

Navigation System XYZ (Sony):
a motion blur in cross-fading enables
different zoom levels to be combined.

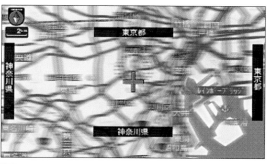

The Fishnet Concept: here, parts of the
content are compressed, which enables
the whole page to be displayed. Search
strings are shown as pop-up menus,
even in the compressed section, and
one can select from them directly.
(Visualisation and Interaction Research
Group at Microsoft Research: Baudisch,
Lee, and Hanna, 2004)

Super Real Tennis (Sega Wow): this
three-dimensional game uses the depth
of the screen and offers a surprisingly
high entertainment quality.

Bigger can be smaller if we take the **resolution** into account. When we refer to a small display, we usually mean its physical size, but the resolution is an additional parameter defining the size of a display. The resolution determines how much information is simultaneously visible on a display. For displays of the same physical size, it can be said that the higher the resolution is, the smaller the rendering of the graphical elements.

Display sizes are often measured in inches. The screen size value is the diagonal length of the display. Pythagoras's theorem is needed to relate the physical dimensions of the screen to the resolution values and the pixel sizes, which are available for display on the screen. Since small screens can be found in so many different formats, the length of the diagonal is no longer a helpful indicator of display size.

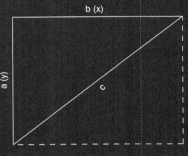

Pythagoras's theorem: $a^2 + b^2 = c^2$

Resolution and physical size of the graphical elements on a screen.

	72 dpi	108 dpi	144 dpi	216 dpi
16 x 16 px				
32 x 32 px				
64 x 64 px				
128 x 128 px				

When **locating a point** on a display, the origin of the coordinate axes is the left hand, top-most corner of the screen. Every distance on the screen is measured from this point.

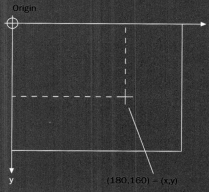

Measuring distance on a display

Glossary

DPI (Dots Per Inch): a measure of the scanning resolution of an image or the quality of an output device. DPI expresses the number of dots that a printer can print, or that a monitor can display, per inch.

PPI (Pixels Per Inch): interchangeable with DPI.

LPI (Lines Per Inch): refers to the quality of a halftone screen in printing. It is important to distinguish LPI from DPI. The LPI is commonly considered to be half the value of the DPI value of the device or image, for example, 300 dpi would equal 150 lpi.

PX (pixel): contraction of picture element. A pixel is the smallest element that display software can use to create text or graphics. A display resolution described as being 640×480 can display 640 pixels across the screen and 480 down the screen, thus providing a total of 307,200 pixels. The higher the number of pixels, the higher the screen resolution.

TFT (Thin Film Transistor): the highest quality and brightest LCD colour display type. A method for packaging one to four transistors per pixel within a flexible material that is the same size and shape as the LCD display, so that the transistors for each pixel lie directly behind the liquid crystal cells that they control.

Active-matrix Display: a type of flat-panel display found on most laptop computers. Active-matrix technology differs from 'passive matrix' only in as much as the screen is refreshed more frequently, creating much better picture quality and better viewing angles. The most common type of active-matrix screen is called TFT (or Thin Film Transistor). The two terms are often used synonymously.

OLED (Organic Light-Emitting Diode): the diodes in displays made with OLEDs emit light when a voltage is applied to them. The pixel diodes are selectively turned on or off to form images on the screen. This kind of display is brighter, thinner and faster than the normal liquid crystal display (LCD) in use today. It also needs less power to run, offers higher contrast, looks just as bright from all viewing angles and is a lot cheaper to produce than LCD screens.

Screens are defined both by their physical size and the number of pixels they can display. The ratio of dots per inch (dpi) is referred to as the resolution of the display. So if we want to define what small screens are, a combination of these two parameters must be taken into account.

Today a screen is considered 'small' if it supports fewer than 307,200 pixels. This is equal to a resolution of 640 x 480 pixels (VGA; see facing page), or a diagonal screen size of approximately 11 inches at 72 dpi.

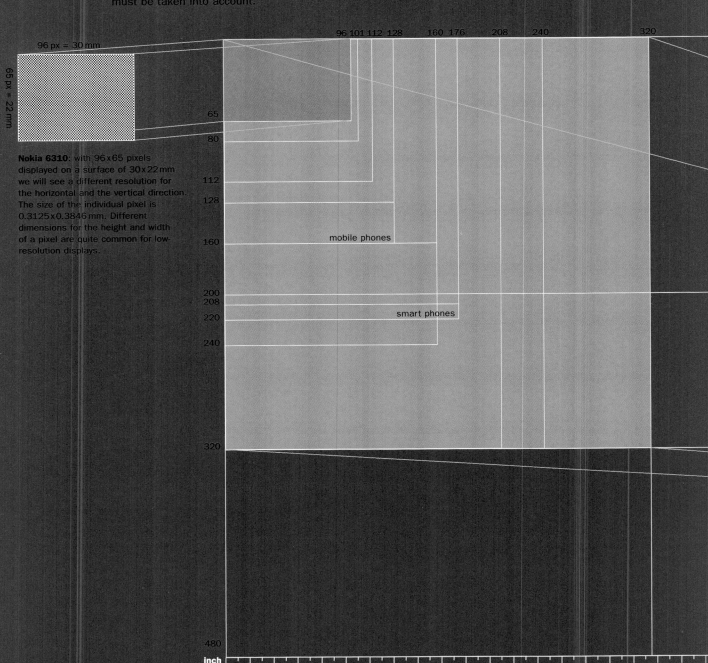

96 px = 30 mm

65 px = 22 mm

Nokia 6310: with 96 x 65 pixels displayed on a surface of 30 x 22 mm we will see a different resolution for the horizontal and the vertical direction. The size of the individual pixel is 0.3125 x 0.3846 mm. Different dimensions for the height and width of a pixel are quite common for low-resolution displays.

96 101 112 128   160 176   208   240   320

65
80
112
128

mobile phones

160

200
208
220

smart phones

240

320

480

inch   1   2   3   4   5

The actual resolution value is growing steadily.
While 72 dpi used to be considered the standard,
resolutions of 144 dpi are quite common today;
especially amongst smaller screens. We can expect
to see even higher resolutions in the future, and the
individual pixel will soon be beyond the capacity of
the human eye.

The qualities of different screens are
denoted by a number of upper case
abbreviations. Each letter represents
a type of functionality, and the list
of letters increases in line with the
screen resolution.

V=Video, **G**=Graphics, **A**=Array, **W**=Wide,
Q=Quarter/Quad, **C**=Colour, **E**=Enhanced,
S=Super, **X**=Extended, **U**=Ultra

4:3	QQVGA	160 x 120				
4:3	QVGA	320 x 240				
16:5	CGA	640 x 200				
64:35	EGA	640 x 350				
4:3	VGA	640 x 480	16:9	WVGA	852 x 480
4:3	SVGA	800 x 600	16:9	WSVGA	1024 x 600
4:3	XGA	1024 x 768	15:9	WXGA	1280 x 768
			16:10	WXGA+	1280 x 800
5:4	SXGA	1280 x 1024	16:9	WSXGA	1600 x 1024
4:3	SXGA+	1400 x 1050	16:9	WSXGA+	1680 x 1050
4:3	UXGA	1600 x 1200	16:10	WUXGA	1920 x 1200
4:3	QXGA	2048 x 1536			
4:3	QSXGA	2560 x 2048	16:9	WQSXGA	3200 x 2048
4:3	QUXGA	3200 x 2400	16:10	WQUXGA	3840 x 2400

480   640 px at 72 dpi

inch

1

2

communicators

3

320 px = 56.4 mm

320 px = 56.4 mm

4

5

Palm Zire 71: at a resolution of 144 dpi
we find 320 x 320 pixels on a surface
of 56.4 x 56.4 mm. The actual size of a
pixel here is 0.16 x 0.16 mm.

6

.... 72 dpi
----------------------- 144 dpi

handhelds

cm
inch   1 inch = 2.54 cm

6   7   8

2A   2B   2C

Passive Matrix

TN
Twisted Nematic
STN
Super Twisted Nematic
FSTN
Film-compensated Super Twisted Nematic

LCD
Liquid Crystal Display (1971)

Active Matrix

TFD
Thin Film Diode
MIM
Metal Insulator Metal

TFT
Thin Film Transistor
P-Si
Polycrystalline Silicon
CGS
Continuous Grain Silicon

ELD
Electroluminescent Display

OLED
Organic Light-emitting Diode

LED
Light-emitting Diode

PLED
Polymeric Light-emitting Diode

Display

CRT
Cathode Ray Tube (1897)

bigger screens

FED
Field Emission Display (1966)

PDP
Plasma Display Panel (1964)

VFD
Vacuum Fluorescent Display (1965)

Electronic Paper
Technology developed by e-Ink (1999)

Smart Paper
Technology developed by Gyricon (1973)

E-paper
Electronic Paper (1973)

Paper-like Display
Technology developed by Canon (1996)

Electronic Particulate
Technology developed by Bridgestone (2002)

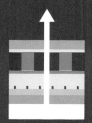   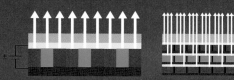

transmissive   reflective   transflective

LCD: liquid crystal displays do not generate any light. Instead the display can be illuminated either by reflecting light from the environment, or by a light source positioned behind the display. It is also possible to combine these two principles; the rear lighting of LCD displays is not yet bright enough to be clearly legible in bright sunshine, but it can be blinding when it is used in the dark. This can be compensated by a brightness sensor and separate darker graphics for use by night.

OLED: organic light-emitting diodes have the advantage that they generate light themselves. This makes them much flatter, brighter and less expensive than LCDs.

SOLED: stacked organic light-emitting diodes lay the three colours of the additive colour mixtures one over the other, which makes the colour rendering more precise and the resolution much finer.

	suited to large screens	size	resolution	full colour	display quality	power consumption	brightness	weight	thickness	lifetime	cost	usage	+ positive • ok − needs improvement
LCD	+	•	+	•	•	+	+	+	+	+	$$$	calculators, TVs, mobile phones, digital cameras, monitors	+ long life − expensive, not optimised for movies
ELD	+	•	+	−	+	−	•	•	+	+	$$	word processors, car navigation systems, monitors	+ high visibility, quick response − difficult to show full colour
OLED	+	•	+	•	+	+	+	+	+	−	$$	mobile phones, PDAs, digital cameras	+ bright, wide viewing angle, thin − short life
LED	−	−	•	−	•	−	+	•	•	•	$	public signs (outdoor), traffic signals	+ long life, high luminosity − light distribution is not uniform
CRT	+	+	+	+	+	•	+	−	−	•	$	public signs (indoor), TVs, monitors	+ best resolution − volume, weight, depth
PDP	+	+	•	−	•	−	•	−	•	−	$$$	TVs, monitors	+ improving resolution − small sizes tend to be dark
VFD	•	•	•	•	•	−	•	−	•	•	$$	car dashboards, audio, neon signs	+ transform free, quick response − high power consumption, noise

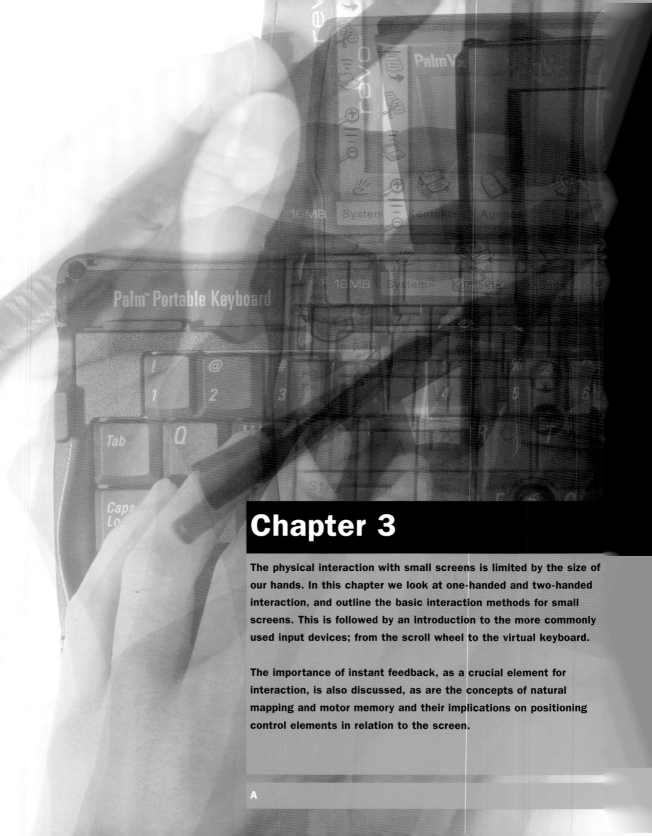

Chapter 3

The physical interaction with small screens is limited by the size of
our hands. In this chapter we look at one-handed and two-handed
interaction, and outline the basic interaction methods for small
screens. This is followed by an introduction to the more commonly
used input devices; from the scroll wheel to the virtual keyboard.

The importance of instant feedback, as a crucial element for
interaction, is also discussed, as are the concepts of natural
mapping and motor memory and their implications on positioning
control elements in relation to the screen.

A

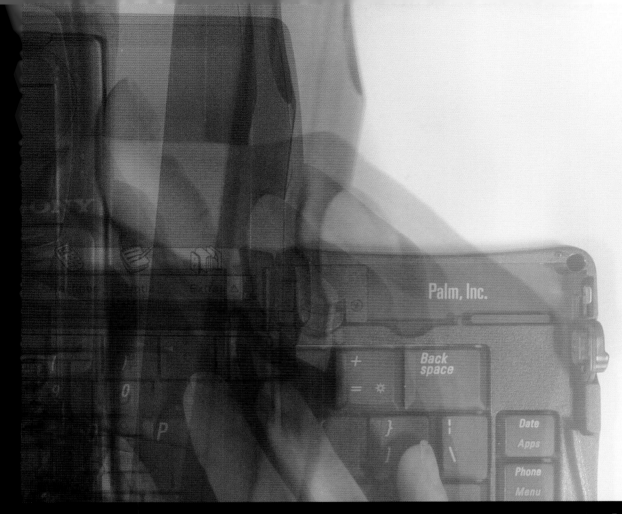

Physical Interaction

The second part of this chapter shows how natural mapping and instant feedback are actually used in interaction applications. This is followed by a review of both the predominant interaction methods and some lesser known, but creative, ways of physical interaction.

In the last section of this chapter we look at the technical side of physical interaction. We explain and visualise the different ways in which a screen can detect where and when it has been touched by the user. Finally, we look at the human side of sensory technology.

B

C

The nature of user interaction plays a far more important role in the design of applications for small-screen devices than in the design of applications for desktop computers. This is partly because there are fewer standardised forms of input or, more simply, no clear equivalent to the keyboard and the mouse. In addition, the context for small-screen device use is far less predictable than for a conventional desktop computer. Even the comparatively mobile use of a laptop computer requires the user to be in a static, seated position. For those portable devices that are often more peripheral in their use, the design options for the menu structures and screen layout will depend far more on the user's likely interaction style.

Physical interaction

Interaction with small-screen devices reveals the conflict of interests between creating the smallest physical size that will give the user unrestricted mobility and flexibility, whilst maintaining dimensions that are defined by the size and the motor functions of the human hand. The balance is not always achieved and some devices are already smaller than the minimum size that can be comfortably operated by an adult hand.

There are two fundamental types of physical interaction that can be distinguished: one-handed and two-handed interaction. Some devices can only be operated with two hands, for example, the Game Boy, whilst other devices offer different modes that can be selected alternately. Smart phones, for example allow the user to dial numbers with one hand, but interaction for more complex applications such as using the calendar or accessing the internet is done with two hands.

Game consoles require two-handed operation, with the use of the thumb and index finger. The hands of the Nintendo generation – used to interacting with game consoles from an early age – have advanced motor skills. For example, it has been observed that young people's thumbs have developed greater sensitivity and motor skills over recent years, and as such the ability of their thumbs is now close to the finely tuned motor skills of their index finger.
(Game Boy Advance)

One-handed interaction enables a device to be used at the same time as carrying out other activities. One-handed interaction presents the greatest challenge for the interaction designer because the same hand is used for the interaction and to hold the device. This means that all fingers, except for the thumb, have restricted freedom of movement, and thus less scope for interaction. Yet the thumb has considerably less fine motor control than the index finger.

In one-handed interaction, a tabulator system is almost always adopted: the user employs their thumb to control a mini joystick, which enables them to move from one menu item to the next and then to confirm their choice. The mini joystick is almost always placed centrally on the front of the device. This is not an ergonomically ideal position, but a compromise so that the device can be operated both with the left and the right hand. However, putting the interactive element in this position does in fact restrict the user's freedom of movement and their ability to navigate the software.

Mobile phones often incorporate one-handed menu interaction, which is controlled through the use of a clickable scroll wheel. (Nokia 7110)

Two-handed interaction often sees one of the hands playing a supporting role so that fine movements, such as data input through use of a stylus or keyboard, are carried out by the other hand.

Full two-handed operation, in which keys and control elements are operated simultaneously with both hands, is mainly found in portable game consoles. Most games focus heavily on the player's fast reactions, so the motor skills of the two hands are used simultaneously. Complex two-handed movement patterns are stored in 'motor memory' so can be called upon as a reflex action when needed. When interaction with a device requires the use of both hands, completing any other activity at the same time is almost impossible, even walking.

Motor memory plays a decisive role in all forms of interaction. Movements stored in this memory can be recalled as reflexes when they are needed. See also 'motor memory' in this chapter.

A **scroll wheel** placed on the side of a device offers ergonomically ideal interaction for the left hand. (Sony CMD X2000)

Interaction techniques and elements

Unlike the standard input methods that evolved for interaction with desktop computers, a multitude of different input and interaction elements have developed for the operation of small, mobile devices.

Sony's 'jogdial' is a **clickable scroll wheel** that can be operated with the thumb. It was one of the first multifunctional elements developed for portable devices. Turning the wheel enables the user to scroll through menu options and pressing the wheel confirms the user's selection. It is usually sufficient to control just the vertical navigation alone because the size, proportions and resolution of the small screen mean that it can only display a simple list. To allow the same element of control with the ability to jump between different hierarchical levels, a knurled wheel was developed that could also be tilted in two directions. The scroll wheel and the knurled wheel have high tactile and motor qualities because they really move, and use of the wheel means that physical stop points can be linked with menu items.

A **jogdial** positioned on the side of a device, which can be tilted to apply extra functions, is almost too difficult for the fine motor skills of the thumb. (Sony CMD Z5)

A **mini joystick** situated in the centre of a device can be reached equally well (or equally badly), by both hands. The position of the interactive elements restricts the thumb's freedom of movement. (Sony Ericsson T610)

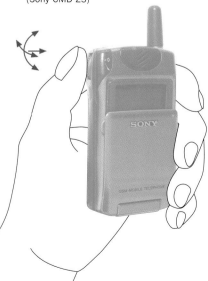

A **mini joystick** is operated with the thumb and can be used to control movements in two directions, and to select items. Pushing the mini joystick in one direction simply defines the direction of the movement; the speed of the movement can be altered by varying the movement of the mini joystick. The mini joystick is cheaper and more robust than a scroll wheel, and therefore became an established interaction component even before the screen sizes and software concepts were really able to incorporate the second direction that it offers.

On small screens there is not yet any representation of the user – in the form of a cursor – so the movement of the mini joystick is not translated into a directional vector; interaction is simply interpreted as a movement that is either horizontal or vertical. Here too, the display jumps from one tabulator to another. The exceptions to this are isolated applications such as navigation systems, in which an extract from a map can be moved obliquely by using the joystick.

Both the scroll wheel and the mini joystick permit one-handed navigation, and sometimes even blind navigation, because the thumb interacts continuously with the same component and does not have to move from one interaction element to another. This means that they are ideal forms of interaction for portable devices because they can be used peripherally. To give the joystick similar tactile and motor qualities to the scroll wheel, techniques such as tactile feedback, e.g. vibration, can be used.

With the **mini joystick**, the movement of the thumb is interpreted as either a vertical or a horizontal movement. The exception is mobile navigation systems.

Apple's rotating **click wheel**, seen on the first generation iPod, displayed direct feedback of the user's movement on the screen, and as such had a high physical quality that contributed significantly to the success of the device. This direct feedback has created a mental model of a virtual transmission, in spite of the fact that the directions of movement are not congruent.

The virtual click wheel is technically little more than a circular touchpad that largely imitates the physical movements of an 'actual' wheel. The virtual click wheel enables the quality of continuous physical interaction to be maintained, but is far cheaper and less prone to error than its actual counterpart. The common element of both wheels is that the user can develop a special skill in their interaction, which is a positive user experience because it helps to foster self-confidence in working with new technology.

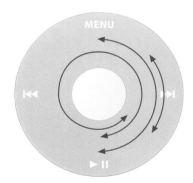

The (virtual) **click wheel** permits highly differentiated interaction. For example, the thumb can turn full circle for fast scrolling, or a more precise selection can be made exactly by making small movements. At the same time, the four quadrants of the pads act as four different selection buttons.

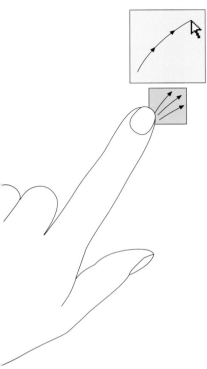

The continuous movement of the cursor is the result of a three-step motion of the user's finger on the touchpad.

The **touchpad**, as an indirect and relative control mechanism, has yet to become established for small screens. The touchpad could be a useful addition to some devices, such as the Pocket PC, but its disadvantage, especially compared to a joystick is that the finger must be moved back and forth several times in order to direct the cursor, which makes one-handed operation difficult.

The **touchscreen** is a very direct and intuitive form of interaction, but on small-screen devices it must be remembered that the finger is a relatively large input instrument. Therefore a stylus is often used for input on small-screen appliances so that the size of interaction elements or icons, and the area of the screen that is obscured during interaction can be reduced. The standard touchscreen does not have any tactile feedback, so the user's eyes must remain on the screen in order to maintain interaction.

In the design of interactive applications for use on a touchscreen, the general rule is that the elements for navigation and interaction should be placed close to the bottom of the screen, so that the screen is unobscured during interaction.

(Palm Vx)

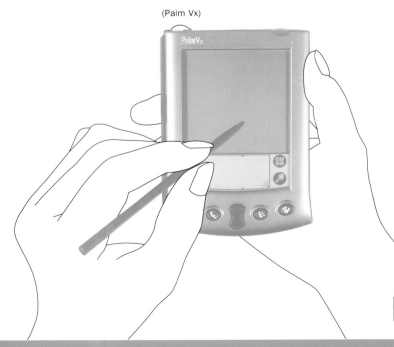

A further technical development of the touchscreen is one that offers tactile feedback. It allows an extra interaction quality and enables the device to be used peripherally. For more information see the example of the Alpine PulseTouch technology in Section 3B.

068|069 >

During the interaction process, conventional touchscreens are unable to distinguish whether the user clicks on the screen or just touches it instead. This means that no balloon help or other rollover effects can be used on touchscreen interfaces. However, the latest generation of touchscreens are able to interpret the pressure of the user's touch, and so can distinguish between rollover and clicking. This progression offers greater scope for the design to include sensitive feedback mechanisms between the actions of the user and the reactions of the device.

In addition to clicking and drag-and-drop interactions, the interpretation of other motions on the touchscreen is becoming increasingly important. For example, a fast zigzag movement can be interpreted as deleting, and circling an object can be interpreted as an expression of interest that zooms in on the corresponding detail.

delete

zoom

home

The **interpretation of gestures** means that the whole of the screen can be used for interaction. The gesture does not need to relate to the image on the screen. Acoustic feedback should be used to reinforce the feedback between the system and the user.

With an **anoto pen** the input problem is reversed; the user can enter data by writing on specially printed paper. The written text or sketch is then transmitted from the stylus to the device. This type of data entry requires a writing surface and full concentration on the writing process, and it is therefore very suitable for certain situations, such as making notes during the course of a meeting.

An anoto pen can use an optical sensor system to transmit the written data to a device by Bluetooth. Specially printed paper makes it possible to detect the exact location of the stylus tip. (Sony Ericsson Chatpen CHA-30 & iScribe Digital Graph Pages)

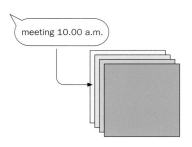

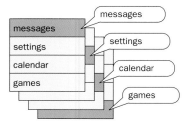

Voice input is very suitable for peripheral use. A technical requirement for voice control at present is a controlled acoustic environment, such as inside a car, so that the system can interpret the input reliably. The dialogue for interaction with a computer-assisted system is still not fluent, so voice input is only effective for short commands or data entries, like e.g. names or addresses. The structural advantage of voice input is that this form of navigation cuts across the hierarchical levels of the overall structure – each menu item can be called up immediately, irrespective of its level within the navigation scheme.

Entering **keywords** by voice input is a fast form of navigation that cuts across the menu hierarchy.

Offering menu choices via **voice output** is an arduous form of interaction and should always be avoided where possible because of the linear character of language. A verbal list of several menu functions is far less effective than a simultaneous visual representation. Yes or no decisions are the only type of interaction dialogue that can be handled at a reasonable speed. Voice output however, is an appropriate technique for delivering content such as e-mails or text messages, because it allows the user to simultaneously carry out other activities, such as driving a car or walking.

The linear character of language makes the selection of **menu functions** time-consuming and arduous.

Advanced design exercise

Define the vocabulary and grammar needed to operate a calculator by voice control.
Try to design the adequate interface of this software by using either visual or acoustic means for the feedback of the device. Try to come up with a persuasive way to demonstrate your concept.

Physical **keys** that are used as interactive elements are especially important for older users because they represent a familiar and reliable way to control a device. Matters can become more complex if these keys have multiple assignments. Soft keys – those keys which are dynamically assigned different functions – should be positioned close to the screen, and the current and active function of the key should always be displayed on the screen. For the successful incorporation of soft keys, the design process of the end device and its interface must be so closely linked that this relationship can be seen at a glance.

The **assignment of physical keys** and their currently active functions should be clearly shown.

The **telephone keypad** with assigned alphabetical letters is a special case of multiple assignment. Using a 12-key block to write long text messages is an arduous task. The automatic word recognition (or predictive text) feature T9 is only helpful in part because it only offers a standard and limited vocabulary. The success of text-based communication between mobile phones is probably due more to the discretion that this form of communication allows, rather than the convenience of its use. In this form of multiple assignment of keys, it is very helpful to have an on-screen display of all of the characters that are represented by any given key when that key is pressed.

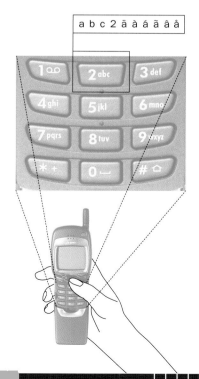

Using the **rotate-and-press** element to enter letters is a particularly arduous input mechanism and only efficient when used to select items from lists.

The size of the **numerical keypad or 'QWERTY' keyboard** is the second factor, alongside the size of the screen, which determines the overall size of the device. That said, there is a limit to just how small a device can be; shrinking beyond a certain point will sacrifice comfort and convenience of use. The keys act as an additional display area, which considerably affects the user's interaction with the device.

Selecting numbers or letters from a list with a single control element, such as a rotate-and-press dial, would be far more complicated than using a keypad, and would place severe restrictions on the speed and convenience of the interaction process. The fact that this principle is used in some devices, for example navigation systems in cars, results from the specific and less than ideal ergonomical situation of the device.

For text input, the discrepancy between the size of the interface needed for optimum user interaction, and the size of the display for visual monitoring is especially great. Folding keyboards are available for PDAs and even for smart phones; they serve to extend the interaction area to a comfortable size, but they also mean that a formerly mobile device is rendered temporarily static.

Folding keyboards are only really effective for keying longer texts, otherwise the installation requires more time than the data entry. (Palm Portable Keyboard)

Additionally there are several variations of **virtual keyboard**. One such type is an input device that is available in the form of gloves, which log and interpret the movements of the fingers. In this concept the display – a keyboard in which the letters are spread out for the user to see – is missing. Use of this virtual keyboard requires that the position of each letter, and its corresponding hand movement, be memorised; a particular typing convention must be followed.

Alternatively, a virtual keyboard can be displayed on the screen or projected on to an external surface. In either case though, interaction with virtual keyboards demands a greater degree of user attention and as such is unsuitable for peripheral use.

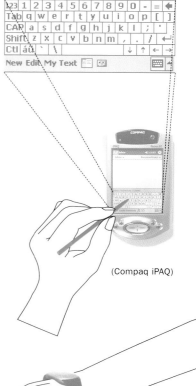

(Compaq iPAQ)

To achieve usability, **virtual keyboards** must offer a display function in which the available letters and functions are shown.
(Senseboard Virtual Keyboard)

This mobile phone is equipped with a **virtual laser keyboard** attachment.
(Siemens SX)

The landscape format of this device is well suited to integrate a **full QWERTY keyboard**.
(Psion revo)

The Blackberry offers a **full QWERTY keyboard** through miniaturisation.
(Blackberry 7230)

All interaction techniques for small-screen devices are subject to the following design principles:
firstly, the system must react to each input command immediately (this is referred to as instant feedback); secondly, the interactive elements should be plausibly arranged in relation to one another and their movement characteristics should be easy to remember (this is referred to as natural mapping); and thirdly, the procedures for use should have high physical and interactive qualities, which can be memorised in the form of finger movements and action sequences (this is referred to as motor memory).

Instant feedback

When designing the interaction scenario or defining which physical actions should trigger which virtual reactions, it must be ensured that the action and the reaction are linked as closely and logically as possible. The period of time between the action and the reaction should also be considered; as far as possible, the system should react in real time to each of the user's actions. This 'instant feedback' provides the user with the feeling that they are directly manipulating and controlling the system. Any delay between the action and the reaction interrupts the user-device dialogue and leads to uncertainty, which can cause the user to incorrectly enter their input again. Communication problems like this will not only frustrate the user, but also place an extra burden on the system – and may cause it to crash.

It is therefore important to design an instant interaction process: each action by the user must be followed immediately by a response from the device. This response could be audible feedback or a subtle visual manipulation of the selected menu item or icon. If the process takes time and requires the user to be patient, there should be some indication of the delay. If there is likely to be a long delay, then the user must be given as much information as possible about the expected waiting time.

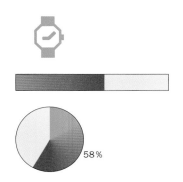

Where there is a **delay in response**, for example, due to loading times, the device should give precise information about what is happening and how long the delay will last.

Subtle but continuous **acoustic feedback** could be used to maintain an instant interaction dialogue between the user and the device.

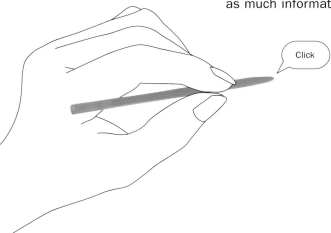

Click

Natural mapping: the position of control elements in relation to the screen

The functional assignment of interaction elements – both physical and virtual – should be logically geared towards the expectations of the user. Where elements are arranged horizontally, the reading direction from left to right should be taken into account. This means that functions such as 'confirm' and 'next' should be on the right of the screen, and functions such as 'back' and 'change' should be on the left. Additional functions or options such as 'further information' should remain neutral in relation to their direction and placement. The vertical axis is semantically linked with the concept that 'up' equals more and 'down' equals less. This can be applied, for example, to functions such as volume and zoom control. When designing soft keys, which have dynamically applied functions, care must be taken to ensure that the assignment of the physical keys is consistent, for example the 'cancel' functionality will always be assigned to the same physical key. The link between the key and the screen should also be as consistent, close and unambiguous as possible.

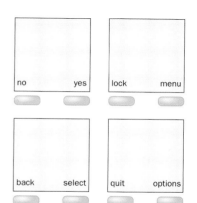

The **reading direction** from left to right naturally indicates that the right key should be assigned to 'confirm' or 'yes', the left key to 'reject' or 'no' (above). To exchange the placement of these keys is illogical (right).

The **scroll bar** is an exception to the concept of natural mapping: the lower arrow key moves the text upwards, but the extract in view is moved down.

Vertical assignment is simpler: the top key is used to increase the value, the bottom key is used to reduce it.

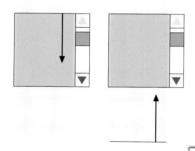

increase	bigger	louder	higher	zoom in	+	▲
decrease	smaller	quieter	lower	zoom out	−	▼

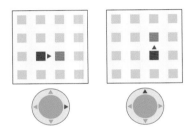

The right **direction key** on the joystick causes the selection on the screen to jump to the right. Similarly the up direction key causes the selection to jump to the row above.

Natural mapping: the movement of the control elements and the accompanying virtual presentation

A logical connection between the physical action and the virtual reaction means that the forms, directions and speeds of the movement should also be designed as congruently as possible. For example, a physical rotation movement should trigger a virtual rotation, and a physical counter-clockwise rotation should generate a virtual counter-clockwise direction. Starting with familiar movement patterns that can be reflected 1:1 in virtual reality and which will work immediately, it is also possible to create other, more complex implementations. For example, a rotating movement in reality can also be plausibly reflected by a linear movement on the screen (a change in the angle of the real movement does not need to be transferred on to the screen as a 1:1 reflection), larger or smaller movements can also be communicated very plausibly and intuitively as long as the system responds in real time so that the action can be corrected at once.

The physical rotating movement can be linked with a **virtual linear movement**. The movement can be interpreted both as a vertical movement and as a horizontal movement: a clockwise turn moves the list upwards and the visible extract downwards. A horizontal movement to the right also corresponds to a clockwise turn.

The link between the user's physical movement and the device's virtual reaction can be translated at **various speeds** by the system.

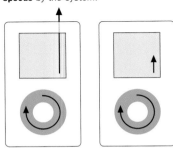

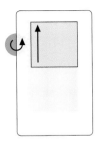

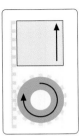

Motor memory

When using devices with small screens, motor memory becomes a particularly important factor. Things that we store in our motor memory represent a fundamental learning experience because they are intrinsically linked to a physical dimension. Many standard usage movements stored in motor memory can be summoned as reflex or 'blind' actions. These sort of actions are often employed in one-handed peripheral use of a device. The nature of this interaction should be taken into account and we should expect interaction concepts that interpret the user's gestures, to become increasingly important in the design process. This means that tactile and auditory interaction should be used as additional feedback wherever possible so that the device can be operated reliably even without looking.

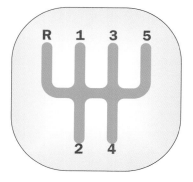

The layout on the gear shift is memorised by the user's motor memory.

The lack of undivided user attention must be taken into account in the development of a small-screen design concept, as subtle design features might be overlooked by the user in peripheral usage situations. See also Chapter 7: Digital Hieroglyphs.

Basic exercise

Test your motor memory:

Which way do you turn a tap to open and close it?

Which way do you turn a screw to tighten or loosen it?

Is it possible to remember these things without carrying out the relevant movement?

The user-friendly design of soft keys is an important task for the interface designer. If designed effectively and efficiently, soft keys provide a means by which the device becomes self-explanatory. This may even go so far as to shorten the user's learning period and may make the operating manual redundant.

W21S (Sony Ericsson, au by KDDI): the position and form enable the elements on the display to be clearly assigned to the respective keys.

W21S (Sony Ericsson, au by KDDI): in calculator mode, all keys on the phone are assigned to special functions, and again in this application they are shown on the screen with their corresponding function.

Left F900C (Toshiba, NTT DoCoMo) and right V601T (Toshiba, Vodafone): if a soft key is temporarily unassigned a function, it can be faded out on the display.

In practice, the interface designer must abide by the formal requirements of the product design in order to create a bridge between the software and the hardware. This requires a creative treatment of the product's design framework with particular regard to the screen layout and the selection of colours and forms.

Rakuraku (Fujitsu, NTT DoCoMo): the position of the soft keys on the screen differs from their corresponding position on the hardware, but the striking form, colours and borders help the user to link them by mental association.

ø 63 mm

Pocket Pate: was developed as an organisational tool for brain-damaged patients. On this device, all information and interaction steps are arranged in a circular form, similar to a clock face. The twelve-part ring of soft keys represents a direct link between the physical keys and the virtual display. (Anne Grüngreiff, 2002)

N1 (Neonode): a cross-shaped control unit is used for the main navigation. The numbers and letters of the N1 can be displayed as a virtual screen keypad when needed. This concept allows the size of the device to be reduced significantly because the physical keypad is not needed. (176 x 220 pixels)

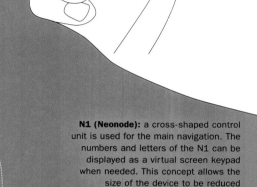

For further information about visual links between hardware and software, see Chapter 8: Layout and Colour on Small Screens.

3A   3B

Text input is now an expected and indispensable function of portable devices. A large number of solutions have been implemented, as can be seen by the examples here, but a universal standard has yet to be established.

Saitek mini keyboard: connects to an iPAQ 3800/3900 Pocket PC.

Tungsten C: this palm handheld PC has an integrated keyboard. This solution means that the device is always used in the same position. Text input can be achieved with one or both hands.

Full-screen keyboard (Spb): the whole display area of this screen keyboard is used for text input. When in text input mode, the device is operated in landscape format with two hands.

58 mm x 77 mm

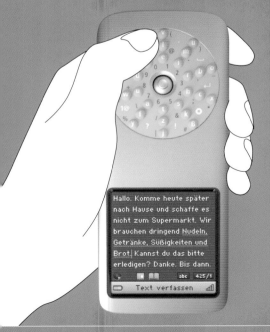

Circular Keyboard Touchpad: In this concept study the alphabet is arranged on a circular touchpad and the position of the keys reflect the access frequency of the letters within a language. The keypad is located above the screen to improve ergonomic handling.

The tactile surface of the pad allows the user to either activate a single letter or to use the surface as a circular touchpad to browse through sub-menus to further edit the text. (Design study Susanne Stage 2005)

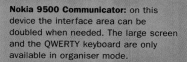

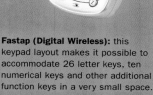

Nokia 9500 Communicator: on this device the interface area can be doubled when needed. The large screen and the QWERTY keyboard are only available in organiser mode.

Siemens SK 65: this mobile phone contains a full QWERTY keyboard. By twisting the top and bottom parts, the keyboard can be used for two-handed text entry.

Fastap (Digital Wireless): this keypad layout makes it possible to accommodate 26 letter keys, ten numerical keys and other additional function keys in a very small space.

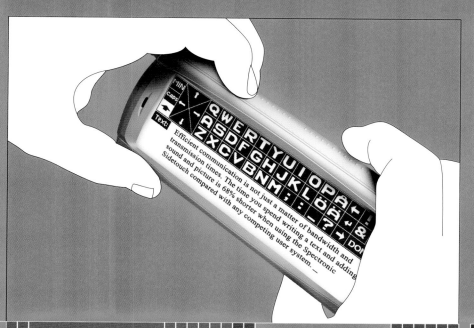

Sidetouch Multimedia Telephone TS 2200 (Spectronic): contains a touchpad on the side of the device that is roughly the same size as the screen. The interaction is logically connected: the front edge of the keypad corresponds to the left edge of the display, and the rear edge of the keypad corresponds to the right edge of the screen. The device can be operated either in portrait or landscape format. The advantage of separating the interaction area and the screen is that the fingers do not obscure the display, and the content can still be directly addressed. (640 x 200 pixels)

The user's interaction with the hardware and the subsequent reaction of the software, can be designed more consistently if work on the concept and development of the hardware and software is carried out at the same time. This enables products to be developed that are a physical pleasure to use. This quality is a decisive factor for success in the marketplace as these devices are no longer just working tools, they are also entertainment machines, and as such the 'fun' factor is an important and additional criterion to the basic ergonomic design.

Apple iPod: the circular movement of the iPod's click wheel is converted into a vertical movement.

The feedback between the input and the reaction on the screen is very precise; both in the mechanical wheel of the first generation iPod and in the electronic touchpad version of subsequent models. When the user navigates the menu, the sub-options are always pushed in from the right. This places the various navigation levels in a spatial context.

The physical pleasure of the controls and the fast reaction of the display animations form an attractive contrast to the dry text-based navigation. (160 x 128 pixels, 2-inch screen)

This system (right), avoids long manual text input by using a built-in camera as a data entry device. By taking a picture of a barcode the mobile phone is able to capture the correct URL of a website. The Japanese provider **au by KDDI** offers a list of websites dedicated to mobile phones.

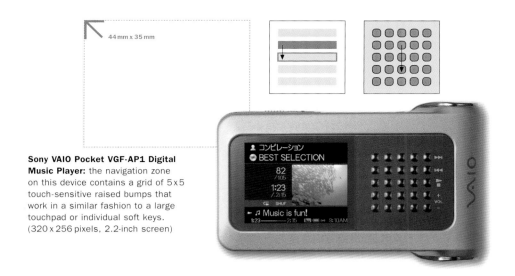

44 mm x 35 mm

Sony VAIO Pocket VGF-AP1 Digital Music Player: the navigation zone on this device contains a grid of 5 x 5 touch-sensitive raised bumps that work in a similar fashion to a large touchpad or individual soft keys. (320 x 256 pixels, 2.2-inch screen)

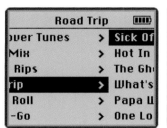

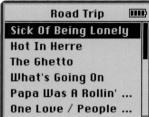

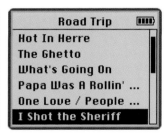

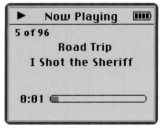

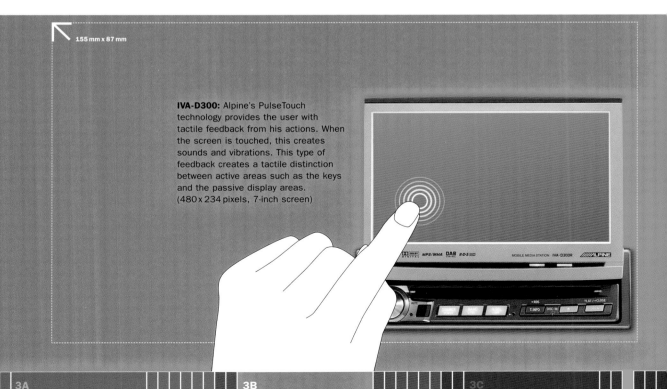

155 mm x 87 mm

IVA-D300: Alpine's PulseTouch technology provides the user with tactile feedback from his actions. When the screen is touched, this creates sounds and vibrations. This type of feedback creates a tactile distinction between active areas such as the keys and the passive display areas. (480 x 234 pixels, 7-inch screen)

Alternative physical forms of interaction that make use of human dexterity and finger agility are especially suitable for small, portable devices. Lower production quantities are economically feasible, which paves the way for a multitude of new product categories. Not all of these new devices are multifunctional, which means that their interaction possibilities need not be as universal as those of the desktop computer; so new and innovative interaction patterns are emerging.

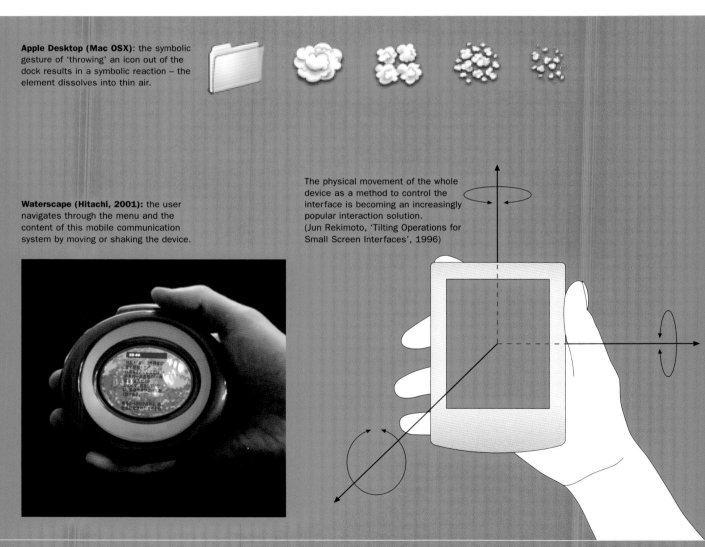

Apple Desktop (Mac OSX): the symbolic gesture of 'throwing' an icon out of the dock results in a symbolic reaction – the element dissolves into thin air.

Waterscape (Hitachi, 2001): the user navigates through the menu and the content of this mobile communication system by moving or shaking the device.

The physical movement of the whole device as a method to control the interface is becoming an increasingly popular interaction solution.
(Jun Rekimoto, 'Tilting Operations for Small Screen Interfaces', 1996)

The **transparent touch display** permits direct interaction with the screen without obscuring the content. If the movement of the fingertip is represented by a cursor, this can also be achieved by use of a separate touchpad and a normal opaque display. (Volker Kaufmann, 2000)

In this study on the **miniaturisation of the keypad**, all keys are brought together on an area that is the size of a thumb. The high-tactile skill of the thumb enables dialling or writing to be carried out with just one hand. (Volker Kaufmann, 2000)

Pustefix: this is an experimental interface for Tetris, a popular computer game. The blocks are rotated and positioned by the user blowing on to the screen. (Johannes Köpp, 2002)

Nintendo DS (2004): this portable game pad is equipped with two touchscreens, which are virtually connected so objects can be moved from one screen to the other. This arrangement permits 'laptop-like' use: the lower horizontal screen is an input medium, and the vertical screen is an output medium. (256 x 192 pixels, 3-inch screens)

61 mm x 46 mm

Wario Ware Touched (Nintendo): this is another interesting form of interaction that includes both sound recording and interpretation: a game is offered that allows the user to interact with Donkey Kong by blowing on to the screen.

Not all **touchscreen technologies** are suitable for all applications. In the design of touchscreen applications, the type of screen as well as the interaction detection technology must be taken into account in order to achieve the best results.

For some applications two of these technological principles are combined to overcome the limitations of a single technology.

Resistive Screen: a flexible layer, coated with a transparent metal oxide, is deformed by pressure and so brought into contact with a secondary layer that is also covered with a conductive coating.

This is a very widespread and relatively inexpensive principle, but the soft, top layer can be damaged by sharp objects. The gap between the two layers causes a slight loss of brilliance and brightness.

These sensory layers are not only able to register pressure, but they can also work in reverse and provide **tactile feedback** by contraction and expansion.

With this further development, interactive elements on the screen can be felt. Up to eight different tactile stimuli can be generated.

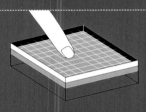

Infrared Screen: infrared light is transmitted across the surface from left to right and from top to bottom, thus creating a matrix. The finger interrupts the ray of light, and in this way, the movement can be assigned to a corresponding coordinate on the screen.

This principle also works if the user is wearing a glove, but not if using a stylus. The system is very sensitive, and it may be activated if dirt or other alien objects interrupt the infrared light. The parallax of the glass layer can limit the accuracy.

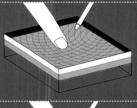

Surface Acoustic Wave (SAW) Screen: here, acoustic waves are transmitted across the surface. The finger will interrupt these waves and allow the interaction to be localised.

The principle offers a brilliant image display and as such is a robust structure, which is often found in kiosks and information terminals. It can also be operated if the user is wearing a glove, but it is sensitive to dirt.

Capacitive Screen: a conductive, transparent layer registers touch because it changes the voltage. Sensors at the edges of the display determine the position.

This principle also offers a brilliant image and is not sensitive to dirt, but it is not scratchproof. It cannot be operated with a glove, instead a special stylus is needed to operate it.

Capacitive-projected Screen: here, a second layer of glass is used. A matrix of conductive, transparent metal oxide enables the touch to be localised.

This system can also be operated with a glove. It has a thicker glass layer, and is therefore a particularly robust system that works under extreme conditions.

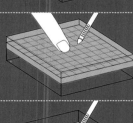

Inductive Screen: in this principle, the sensory layer is situated behind the LCD display. This principle provides a very brilliant image, but it only works with a specially equipped stylus.

Human perception occurs in a highly complex manner via an assessment of **sight, sound, smell, taste** and **touch**. The latter sense, also known as haptic perception, represents a combination of many different sensual elements. These include the tactile sensors that detect **pain, pressure, temperature** and **vibrations**, and the kinesthetic sensors that detect, **contact pressure, muscle tension** and the **angle of the body joints**.

The human body is not evenly equipped with receptors for each of these types of perception. The fingertips have the highest concentration of pressure receptors; over 20 per square millimetre, but the back has the lowest concentration of these receptors; here, the gaps between the receptors are several centimetres.

Sensory perception also specialises in detecting changes. Receptors become accustomed to permanent stimuli and then only react when these parameters change, because a change may signify danger or an opportunity. For this reason we can become accustomed to a permanent noise level or an unpleasant smell as it will cease to be consciously perceived. However, it must be assumed that suppressing, or filtering out, this perception happens actively and is therefore tiring.

Highly-tuned **motor skills** are needed to handle electronic devices, and this presents a special opportunity for communication with small interfaces; the designer cannot rely on the power of visual communication alone. Due to the small size of the display and the distractions of the visual information in the environment, it is advisable to first transmit the information in a redundant way, such as the vibration alarm on a mobile phone, and secondly to establish handling rituals that draw on human motor skills, so that the user does not need to look at the screen constantly.

The sense of sight is a passive input channel, which is like the senses of sound, smell and taste. The difference, compared with the other senses, is that sight can process far more information simultaneously. Using sight as an output channel, for example in eye control, is only useful in very specific applications in which the hand cannot be used.

The human hand is a multifunctional tool, and the action of the thumb and index finger is very sophisticated. The hand is both a very efficient and complex sensor system, as well as a sensitive and highly mobile gripping implement. This combination makes it a very sensitive input/output system and a knowledge tool and this is even reflected in our language -- when we speak of 'grasping' something, we are really talking about the mental process of understanding.

The human feet are also fairly well equipped in their sensory and motor abilities. However, this capacity is greatly limited by wearing shoes.

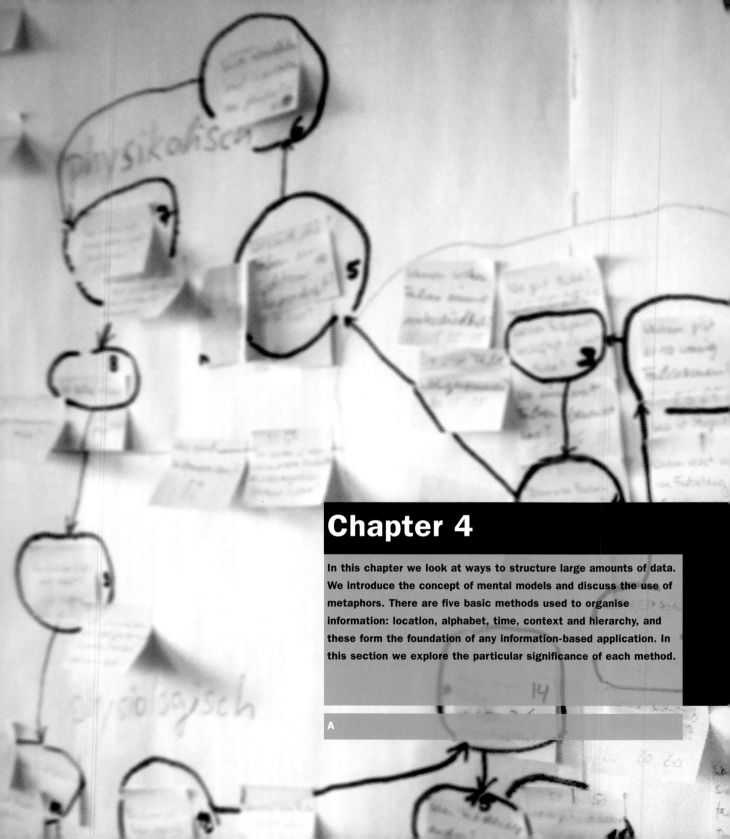

Chapter 4

In this chapter we look at ways to structure large amounts of data. We introduce the concept of mental models and discuss the use of metaphors. There are five basic methods used to organise information: location, alphabet, time, context and hierarchy, and these form the foundation of any information-based application. In this section we explore the particular significance of each method.

A

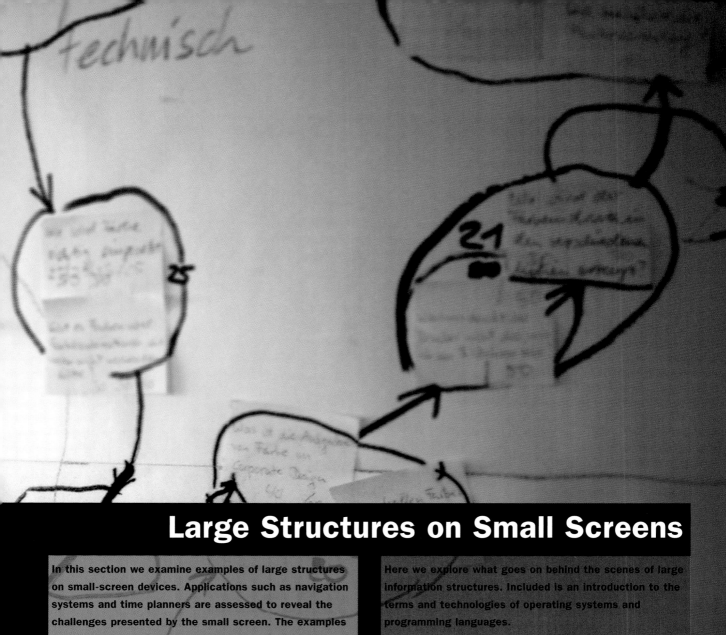

Large Structures on Small Screens

In this section we examine examples of large structures on small-screen devices. Applications such as navigation systems and time planners are assessed to reveal the challenges presented by the small screen. The examples demonstrate creative ways to overcome the inherent shortcomings of a small device.

Here we explore what goes on behind the scenes of large information structures. Included is an introduction to the terms and technologies of operating systems and programming languages.

B

C

Large software structures can be very complex and extensive. The more generic the hardware is, the greater the number of applications that can be installed and used on it. However, this means that it is no longer possible to create an unambiguous link between the physical form, the interaction concept and the software application. Instead the interaction concepts must be made more general so that they can be used in a large number of different applications. The visual interface of the screen is all the more important because it must enable the user to understand the interaction concept for each program and provide the relevant operating instructions.

The mental model

It is important to convey a mental model that allows the user to visualise the 'invisible' space inside the device, this means that the user can gain an impression of the structure of the system. To create this sort of mental model the rules within the system must be plausible, easy to learn and the user must be able to rely on the rules once they have learned them.

Visualisations of the data in the form of maps and diagrams can serve as a basis for a mental model. This type of presentation enables meaningful links and logical interrelationships to be displayed – in a similar fashion to the results of a mind-mapping exercise. Later these models help with more detailed control because the user has already developed a basic concept of the overall system structure. For example, if a device needs operating instructions then some form of synchronous visualisation of these instructions should be employed, and ideally the main navigation level should offer the user any necessary explanations and instructions.

A mental model does not need to correspond with the actual structure of the software. Often, the user interface is a more simplified model of, or metaphor for, the processes that actually occur. Alan Kay, the inventor of the graphical user interface, calls this the 'user illusion'. The ability to form an appropriate mental model of the way a device works depends, to a large extent, on the user's experience in working with electronic devices.

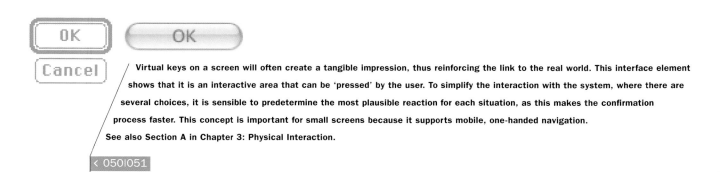

Virtual keys on a screen will often create a tangible impression, thus reinforcing the link to the real world. This interface element shows that it is an interactive area that can be 'pressed' by the user. To simplify the interaction with the system, where there are several choices, it is sensible to predetermine the most plausible reaction for each situation, as this makes the confirmation process faster. This concept is important for small screens because it supports mobile, one-handed navigation.
See also Section A in Chapter 3: Physical Interaction.

< 050|051

The human ability to learn is characterised by the creation of a link with what is already known, and the transference of this knowledge to new situations. This principle is important as it means that the designer must know the intended target audience for a product when selecting its structure, in order to ascertain what likely prior knowledge and experience the potential user can call upon.

The **context-sensitive cursor** is a good way to give the user specific navigation hints or instructions. However, this feature is only possible if there is a pointer element for navigation.

The **dustbin** is often used as a metaphor for the 'delete' function. This metaphor is so easy to understand that it has been in use for 30 years. It is sensible, especially in a drag-and-drop environment, because it embodies the instruction for interaction: if a file is dragged on to this symbol, it is deleted. It is also possible for the user to change his mind, because files can also be retrieved from the dustbin.

The metaphor is a practical form of the mental model. The metaphor, which is reflective of the human learning, starts with the familiar and transfers this to a new environment. The metaphor forms a narrative framework in which to place the possibilities within the system into a context that is logical for the user. Objects and actions are often borrowed from the real world to illustrate similar functions of the system.

The metaphor of the desktop, for example, enabled computers with this graphical user interface to be used for the first time by people with little or no knowledge of computers. The transfer of everyday objects and processes from the classical office environment and on to the interface allowed users to draw conclusions about the functions and the type of interaction that they offered. Equally, the interface of a pocket PC is closely based on structures that are recognisable from larger PCs, and as such it connects with the mental model that is already familiar to the user.

The concept of files that can be saved in folders, which can then be used to create new filing structures, has also become established in many systems. An **enclosing metaphor,** which defines the idea of the working environment in greater detail would actually be a hindrance, because it would transfer real space restrictions into virtual reality.

Metaphors can be a disadvantage. The metaphor as a closed narrative framework has not become established, and nor has a separate, all-embracing metaphor for small-screen devices. Instead, a number of single metaphorical interface elements have become established, such as the button, the folder, the magnifying glass or the dustbin. This is partly due to the fact that closed metaphors are difficult to scale, but a larger problem is the naturalism of metaphors: many functions of a digital system do not have any corresponding function in the real world, as such no metaphorical counterpart can be found.

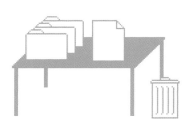

```
▼  📁 new folder 1
   ►  📁 new folder 1.1
   ►  📁 new folder 1.2
   ►  📁 new folder 1.3
   ▼  📁 new folder 1.4
      ►  📁 new folder 1.4.1
      ▼  📁 new folder 1.4.2
         ►  📄 new file1.4.2.1
   ►  📁 new folder 1.5
   ►  📁 new folder 1.6
►  📁 new folder 2
►  📁 new folder 3
►  📁 new folder 4
►  📁 new folder 5
►  📁 new folder 6
```

Nested lists work on small screens if the tabulator offset is kept to a minimum. This structure allows one-handed scrolling through all levels of navigation, without any need for a 'back button'.

Context

An important factor when considering orientation within large data structures is the preservation of context. The length of a book can be determined by the thickness of the its spine, however the size of a digital application is far more difficult to estimate. Equally if you look at any page in an open book, you can easily determine where you are within the progression of that book, but orientation within a digital application is far more difficult. The designer should therefore always try to give the user guidance and placement orientation. One way of doing this is to make several hierarchical levels visible at the same time. This gives the user a better idea of the structure and content as well as their position within the system.

Various display techniques have been established to show several hierarchical levels simultaneously. For example, a nested list is one way to show the tree structure of a hierarchy, or a preview of files in the form of thumbnails might correspond to a simultaneous display of the navigation and content levels. In the implementation of such concepts, small screens present a special challenge because of the limited available space. A zoom function, especially a distorted zoom, can help to make economical use of the space.

Thumbnails enable files to be viewed without opening them. This is another concept that links navigation and content levels, and therefore makes interaction easier and more convenient.

On small-screen devices, techniques that **stretch or condense the content**, depending on the focus, can be used for long lists or large tables such as calendars.

Analogue and digital

When numbers are presented on a small screen, an analogue display is preferable to a digital display. Diagrammatic visualisation can provide the contextual information that enables the displayed value to be interpreted. This applies not only to information that is familiar to the user, such as the time, but also to parameters with values and units which are less familiar or unknown. The numeric display of the current loading speed in megabytes per second is less helpful than a bar diagram that shows approximately how long the process will take and how far it has already progressed. The same applies to the signal strength, the charge status and the volume control. In each case, visualisation can show minimum and maximum values and thus display the current value in a meaningful context, which makes the interpretation easier and faster. Other applications that are suitable for analogue visualisation are file size, available memory space and call charges.

Only if display space is available should non-essential information, which allows a higher degree of precision, be added. For example, combining a visual display such as a loading bar and adding a time estimate can help the user to make a more qualified decision whether or not to download a file.

Visualising the abstract data, preferably within the range of values, creates easy-to-grasp information.

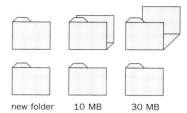

new folder   10 MB   30 MB

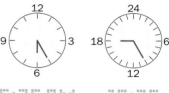

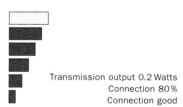

Transmission output 0.2 Watts
Connection 80 %
Connection good

Volume 40 dB
Volume 60 %

Download rate 100 Kbps
60 % received
12 MB of 20 MB received
Remaining time 24 minutes

Preview options for the content can be displayed temporarily. This preserves the context and means that the decisions made on the next steps of navigation can be more informed. For other techniques to make maximum use of the screen space, see Section A in Chapter 2.

Organising information

According to the information architect Richard Saul Wurman, there are five different categories that can be used to organise information, these are: **location, alphabetical order, time** (sequence), **category** (context of meaning) and **hierarchy**.

In computer-aided systems, the designer does not need to decide which of these classifiers is the right one for the content that needs to be organised. The designer can instead use several organisational criteria, because the system is able to reorganise all data at any time and in accordance with any predetermined category. This means that the same information can be presented again and again, but in different contexts, and this functionality can help the user to find and retrieve specific data with ease.

In the digital medium, redundancy is positive. The anticipated questions and expectations of the user should define the principles by which data is to be organised. When determining these, the designer can make use of the fact that the medium is able to respond to different user types and needs by supporting redundant navigation paths. In return, the designer must decide what meta-information should be included in a file.

These 16 cities can be organised by very **different principles**. Depending on the user's question, the data can be arranged in different ways. Sorting in alphabetical order is useful for large volumes of data, but it does not help to answer questions such as:
Where is Rome?
Which city is the oldest?
What language is spoken in this city?
Which city is the largest?
Which city has most inhabitants?

Location: geographical position

Basic design exercise

Develop an organisational structure for your music collection. Try to develop a system for each of the five organisational principles (LATCH), and then evaluate which of these concepts could be combined effectively for a more specific application.

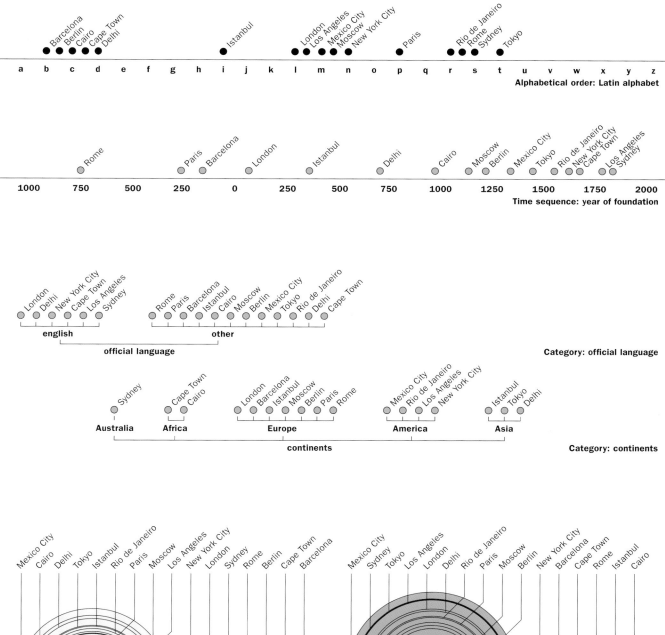

Barcelona Berlin Cairo Cape Town Delhi

Istanbul

London Los Angeles Mexico City Moscow New York City

Paris

Rio de Janeiro Rome Sydney Tokyo

| a | b | c | d | e | f | g | h | i | j | k | l | m | n | o | p | q | r | s | t | u | v | w | x | y | z |

Alphabetical order: Latin alphabet

Rome · Paris Barcelona · London · Istanbul · Delhi · Cairo · Moscow Berlin · Mexico City Tokyo · Rio de Janeiro New York City Cape Town · Los Angeles Sydney

| 1000 | 750 | 500 | 250 | 0 | 250 | 500 | 750 | 1000 | 1250 | 1500 | 1750 | 2000 |

Time sequence: year of foundation

London Delhi New York City Cape Town Los Angeles Sydney — **english**

Rome Paris Barcelona Istanbul Cairo Moscow Berlin Mexico City Tokyo Rio de Janeiro Delhi Cape Town — **other**

official language

Category: official language

Sydney — **Australia**

Cape Town Cairo — **Africa**

London Barcelona Istanbul Moscow Berlin Paris Rome — **Europe**

Mexico City Rio de Janeiro Los Angeles New York City — **America**

Istanbul Tokyo Delhi — **Asia**

continents

Category: continents

Mexico City Cairo Delhi Tokyo Istanbul Rio de Janeiro Paris Moscow Los Angeles New York City London Sydney Rome Berlin Cape Town Barcelona

Hierarchy: area in km²

Mexico City Sydney Tokyo Los Angeles London Delhi Rio de Janeiro Paris Moscow Berlin New York City Barcelona Cape Town Rome Istanbul Cairo

Hierarchy: inhabitants in millions

4A   4B   4C

Location

Sorting by **geographical** location is a powerful form of organisation, as maps offer a very efficient background on which other types of information can also be displayed.

The **real** location as an organisational criterion is increasingly important, especially for portable devices. The ability to find the location of the user and the device, for example, by a global positioning system, reverses the relationship between the hardware and the software – the user becomes a cursor in the real world. Location-based services use the information about the location to simplify the navigation within a software application. Hierarchical levels can be skipped because the geographical context information has already been evaluated. To ensure that this organisational criterion really makes things easier, the integration of the location must not be automatic, otherwise there is a danger that the choice of available options may be restricted.

Location-based services: navigation through the hierarchy is simplified by the fact that the device knows its own location, and includes this in the user guidance. For example, in New York, it will recommend products and services that are located in New York first.

The geographical location can serve as a backdrop for all other information. It can form the mental model into which other information can be saved, such as size, population density, age or native language.

* Year of foundation
▌ Official language
● Area
● Inhabitants

Complex data transactions and relationships can be portrayed in a visual form by **mapping**, and data maps can have similar guidance functions as those of a real geographical map.

Data maps impose spatial situations on abstract content and as such they create meaning. Many concepts in our language use spatial relationships to explain abstract concepts, for example, we may refer to 'background information'. If the data mapping relates to a chronological process, then the mental model can even become a 'roadmap'.

www.waitaki.otago.ac.nz

The **location on the screen** plays a decisive role in a very practical sense, as the display is a surface on which information is localised. The localisation of functions on the screen makes it easier to find them, and thus helps the user to develop a routine in their use of the system.

The designer can also make use of the user's spatial memory in the development of small-screen interface by subdividing the available space on the screen into specific functional zones and areas, and placing tools and navigation aids at the edges of the screen. Spatial memory can also be applied to unseen objects, such as pull-out menus or function bars. To fully make use of spatial memory, the basic functions must always be placed at, or pulled out from, the same point on the screen.

The circular arrangement of selection points is called a **pie menu**. It is much easier for the user to remember angles, rather than the position of an item on a list, as this takes full advantage of their spatial memory.

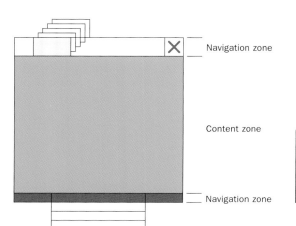

Navigation zone

Content zone

Navigation zone

Human spatial memory should be exploited on small devices by assigning certain functions to a fixed place on the screen. The principle works even if these functions are temporarily pushed off the screen.

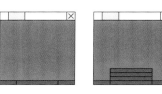

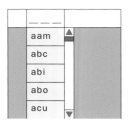 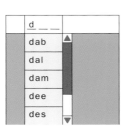 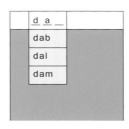 

The principle of **reverse selection** offers the fastest navigation in alphabetical lists.

Alphabetical order

Sorting by alphabetical order is a robust form of organisation. It enables a large number of elements to be made available in a sorted list, and is used particularly for sorting names and lexicographical collections. It is especially useful on small-screen devices to structure long lists via the option to pre-select the first letter. To increase the ease of navigation, it should also be possible to scroll the alphabetical list continuously. If the form of interaction is limited, for example, in small mobile devices or navigation systems in cars, the input can be simplified by reversing the selection principle. For each letter entered, the scrollable list becomes shorter and shorter until the selection is so small that the desired term or name can be seen.

The **starting point** for all chronologically-organised data should be the present.

Time sequence

Organisation by time sequence is an important navigation aid in computer-aided systems. It is essential for users to be able to trace their activities in virtual reality by reconstructing or retracing their actions on the basis of the data trail that they created.

If the **time sequence** is arranged vertically, the latest entry should always be placed at the top. This ensures that any new entry is visible immediately and long scrolling is avoided.

Time sequence can easily be displayed in the form of a list; time context requires a graphical presentation that indicates periods of time and the duration of events. When ordering events by time, the reading direction on the horizontal axis is from left to right: the past is found to the left, and the future to the right. On the vertical axis, the past is viewed at the bottom and the future at the top. In both cases, the present should be the zero point on the scale, and it should be visible when the application is opened.

Category

Organising the content by meaning context is the most subjective of the organisational principles. Here you will find the greatest potential for discrepancy in the perception and evaluation of the content, and there is often a difference between the ideas of the developer and the ideas of the user.

Due to the restricted space on small screens, this discrepancy can force the user to spend a frustrating amount of time looking for their desired function because the structure is split into more hierarchical levels than on larger screens. Organisation by meaning context, which is often the main level of navigation for a software interface, should always be developed in conjunction with potential users or, at the very least, the concepts should be tested with the target users. In familiar applications, it will be important that the subdivision of the content matches the user's already established mental model. In unfamiliar applications, the basic organisational context must be communicated clearly so that the user can create an adequate mental model.

Organising the content by meaning context supports a user's spatial memory, as the concepts developed are often familar to those found in the real world, for example folders and filing systems.

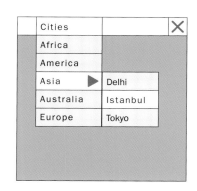

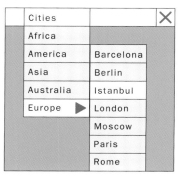

Redundancy is positive: in digital media, the data assignment may be simplified. If the cities are organised by continent, for example, a special case such as Istanbul can be listed under both categories without creating confusion for the user.

Hierarchy

The most common form of hierarchical order is by importance. This organisational principle is however, very subjective, and therefore it can cause the same problems as does arranging the content by meaning context. However, in the case of hierarchical organisation it is possible to derive the user's importance for each item via the frequency of use, and thus change the order dynamically. This principle is very suitable for small-screen devices because it helps to make effective use of the limited space and shortens the navigation paths.

If the relevance of a function is derived by other criteria than the frequency of use, the underlying algorithms can only ever be very incomplete approximations of the complex behaviour of the user. By making small assumptions, however, ease of navigation can be improved, and this is demonstrated by the results listings of websites such as Google and Amazon. Google sorts the search results by the number of links that refer to a site, and Amazon derives patterns from the buying activities of its customers by comparing users with similar interests.

The **hierarchical order** changes with use. The more often a function is called up, the more prominently it is displayed.

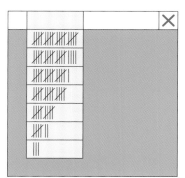

Shallow hierarchies

A decisive factor in determining the intuitive use of an application is whether it is possible for the user to gain a general overview of the system.

Shallow hierarchies are a good way to achieve an overview because they permit a synchronous display of all options available to the user. This is especially relevant for subjects in which the user may find it difficult to follow the logic of the organisational criteria. In such a case, the parallel display of all options can help the user to identify what they are looking for because there is no need to guess which category the term comes under.

However, this advantage of a shallow hierarchy can become a disadvantage if the number of options is so great that they cannot be displayed simultaneously or if the display becomes too confusing. The danger of overloading the interface is one of the main problems in adapting shallow hierarchies to small-screen devices.

In this example of a **shallow hierarchy**, the user moves directly from the navigation level to the content level.

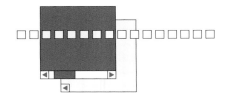

Planning the hierarchy and deciding how steep or shallow the navigation structure should be is a task that the designer should tackle in conjunction with all other disciplines involved in the development process. The hierarchy determines the structure of the underlying data structures, such as databases and searches. It also has a great influence on the design options of the interface, for example, which navigation elements must be available at which point.
Also refer to the planning and visualisation techniques for complex structures in Chapter 9.

156|157 >

Steep hierarchies

Steep hierarchies break down a subject area into a branched structure that is organised by categories. An advantage of this model is that it offers a limited number of options on every level of the hierarchy. On each level, the user must decide which branch of the tree they wish to progress to. The selection is confirmed to move down through the hierarchy. To move back upwards through the structure, a 'back' command is needed.

A steep decision-making pyramid with a branch-like structure is difficult for the user to navigate in complex applications because it can be hard to understand the organisation of the content, and this may lead the user to guess whether the desired content will be found under a certain category. This necessitates a great deal of clicking in order to look inside the available categories, and a 'back' command is required after every wrong guess. This is partly because the hierarchy that a software development engineer considers appropriate may not be in accordance with the user's priorities and their subjective ideas of a hierarchy.

In this example of a **steep hierarchy**, the main navigation level leads to subcategories, and the content within these is then broken down into several further levels.

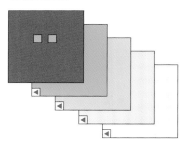

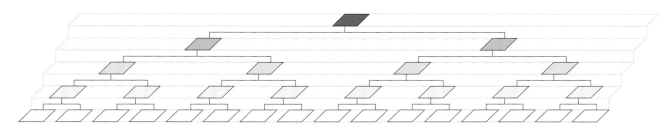

Advanced design exercise

Try to organise all the members of a particular species of mammal.

Is this family-tree hierarchy suitable for use as a structure for an interactive program?

Are there alternative criteria for sorting the animals, that could make a search for

a species easier, such as habitat, size or colour?

Calendar Function on Mobile Phones: the presentation of calendars in small spaces is more or less standardised. The linear progress of time is broken down into separate views, such as months and days, but some of the contextual information is lost in the process. Periods that last longer than about two months are difficult to visualise, and so they are difficult to manage. Equally, showing appointments at the monthly 'zoom level' is a challenge for the designer.

Time-based arrangements are most easily displayed on small-screen devices in the form of tables. The annotations and tables for days, months or public holidays are familiar from printed diaries or calendars and therefore easy to use. The meaning context of years, months, days and hours is so straightforward that navigation between each of these 'zoom levels' works even without further explanation. However, this presentation breaks the time continuum down into discrete steps, which can make it more difficult to present periods and processes.

HP iPAQ RX3000

Panasonic P252IS

Samsung P730

Samsung P730

Palm Zire 21

Nokia 7270

Samsung E610

Samsung E800

Sony Ericsson K700

Philips 755

The ability to **link information about time and location** is a distinct advantage of the digital medium (compared with a conventional desk diary), but synchronous visualisation of this information on small-screen devices is a major challenge.

Activis Scheduler: this concept for an organisational tool enables appointments to be planned and administered in their spatial context. All appointments that are entered in the vertical time bar are also shown in their spatial relationship to each other on the map. This means that the travel can be efficiently planned by ensuring that appointments that are spatially close together are also timed closely together.
(Hendrik Rieß, 2005)

Embedding complex structures into closed **metaphors** is a useful way to support intuitive use. However, this form of closed narrative framework is difficult to scale. This framework is limited when there is a large volume of data, and it is difficult to expand, so new data cannot usually be integrated in a logical way.

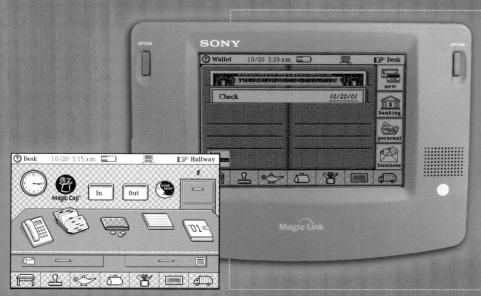

Magic Link PDA/Magic Cap Software (Sony, 1993): this device extends the classic desktop metaphor to include additional functions, such as the internet.

The metaphor is further extended by the addition of further locations, for example, the archive. There is also the possibility of going into town to shop. This metaphor is immediately understood by the user because it is based closely on reality.
(482 x 322 pixels)

The **visualisation of spatial information** is particularly difficult on small screens because context and reference points are always necessary if the user is to get their bearings. The scale of the display must be suffcient enough not only to show enough detailed information, but also enough contextual information. This means that the presentation form, perspective and degree of abstraction must be selected very carefully. If it is not possible to display the information at a single representation scale, a combination of several representations must be considered.

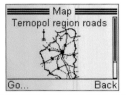
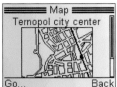
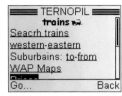

WAP Page (Ternopil): on a small, monochrome mobile phone display it can be very difficult to present large structures in an understandable form.

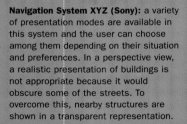

142mm x 85mm

Navigation System XYZ (Sony): this device incorporates a larger screen (6.5 inches), a higher resolution (1458x790 pixels) and the use of colour, and these features allow a much clearer presentation of spatial information. Extra guidance is provided by highlighting prominent buildings.

Navigation System XYZ (Sony): a variety of presentation modes are available in this system and the user can choose among them depending on their situation and preferences. In a perspective view, a realistic presentation of buildings is not appropriate because it would obscure some of the streets. To overcome this, nearby structures are shown in a transparent representation.

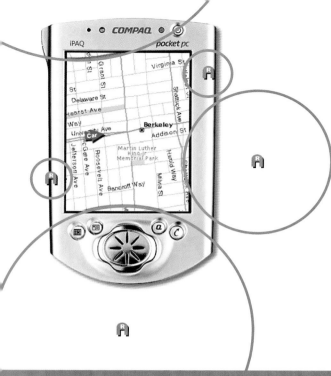

The 'Halo' Concept: usually the extract of a map is so small that destinations which are further away cannot be viewed in the same screen. Use of the halo technique means that destinations outside of the display are represented by a hint of a circle. The circle is the most stable geometrical form, so even a small section of the circumference is enough to indicate the direction and distance of the remote destination. As the viewer moves closer to the destination, the circle becomes smaller and smaller until it is eventually replaced by the destination point.
(Visualization and Interaction Research Group at Microsoft Research: Baudisch and Rosenholtz, 2003)

Navigation System XYZ (Sony): peripheral use of a device in a car is made easier by gesture control. For example, a circular movement to the left zooms the display to the appropriate point, and a movement in the form of a roof takes the user back to the 'home' page.

Gestures can also be used as a form of interaction. See also Chapter 3: Physical interaction.

Navigation System XYZ (Sony): another display option is the rendered perspective model. The system shows the user's travel route by use of virtual yellow road markings. The addition of a bird's-eye view offers a greater preview area and helps the user to interpret the perspective display correctly. The design of the virtual traffic signs is closely based on reality.

4A   4B   4C

	Applications are software programs that can be used on a computer, for example word processing.	Microsoft Office, Adobe Photoshop, Macromedia Flash, Apple Safari
Mac OS / symbian	The **operating system** administers all of the hardware components of a device, controls all processes and routines, and provides the user interface.	Linux, Mac OS, Windows NT, Windows Mobile, Symbian OS, Palm OS, Nokia IPSO

```
BASIC
PRINT "SmallScreen!"

C++
printf("SmallScreen\n");
```

A higher **programming language** works independently of the machine. The instructions can be formulated to address specific problems, and special programs translate the instructions into machine code. This translation can be done line-by-line by use of an **interpreter**, or before the program starts by a **compiler**.

Another distinguishing feature of programming languages is the underlying concept. The three classification concepts are **procedural**, **logical** and **object-oriented programming languages**.

Ada, ALGOL, BASIC, C, C++, COBOL, Delphi, Eiffel, Focus, Fortran, Lingo, Lisp, Modula, Objective-C, Pascal, Python, Visual Basic

Java, Smalltalk

Perl, PHP, SQL

```
Basic's Assembler
ADR    R0, text
SWI    "OS_PrettyPrint"
SWI    "OS_NewLine"
MOV    PC, R14
.text
EQUS   "SmallScreen"
EQUB   0
ALIGN
```

Assembler is a **simple programming language** that is directly related to the physical hardware, such as the processor type on which the program will later be run.

```
0    0000 0000    32    0010 0000
1    0000 0001    64    0100 0000
2    0000 0010    127   0111 1111
4    0000 0100    128   1000 0000
8    0000 1000    129   1000 0001
16   0001 0000    254   1111 1110
17   0001 0001    255   1111 1111
```

Machine code is the binary code, or language, which is understood and implemented by the hardware.

8 **b**it = 1 **B**yte
1 000 Bytes = 1 KB
1 000 000 Bytes = 1 MB
1 000 000 000 Bytes = 1 GB
1 000 000 000 000 Bytes = 1 TB

Circuits form a physical part of the computer. Circuits translate the machine code into on or off signals: 1 = on and 0 = off

The distinction between operating systems and applications enables a range of functions to be extended flexibly; but this modular approach increases both the proportion of redundant processes and the risk of system errors and crashes.

As a result of the development of processor performance, an increasing number of systems are equipped with an operating system. Even small mobile devices are given operating systems that bring their range of functions close to those of a PC. This means that PC applications can now be adapted for small-screen devices.

Powerful programming languages, such as C, are used to write operating systems, applications or robot controls. As processors are becoming more powerful, these languages are increasingly used for microprocessors in embedded systems, although the code that they generate is more general and therefore less economical.

Some programming languages, such as Smalltalk and Java, use a 'virtual machine' for the execution of the program. This means that the applications are independent of the operating system and can be transported like normal files.

In addition to these powerful programming languages, there are also languages that were developed for special applications, such as SQL, which is used to program databases.

The direct adaptation of the hardware is especially economical, and it makes the processes fast. The disadvantage is the awkward programming, which can easily lead to errors. Today's processors largely compensate for the difference in speed between higher programming languages and assembler-generated code.

PCs

Smartphones, Pocket PCs

PDAs, Organisers

Mobile phones

The hardware and software can interact in different ways in small-screen devices, and this affects the design possibilities. The development of portable devices follows the underlying concept of desktop computers, as such there is a trend towards modular concepts, which contain operating systems and applications.

Game consoles

The further the interaction level moves away from the hardware, the slower and more error-prone the system becomes.

The more an application relies on the hardware, the slower and more inflexible the evolutionary development of the software becomes.

Traffic guidance systems, Logistics

Household appliances

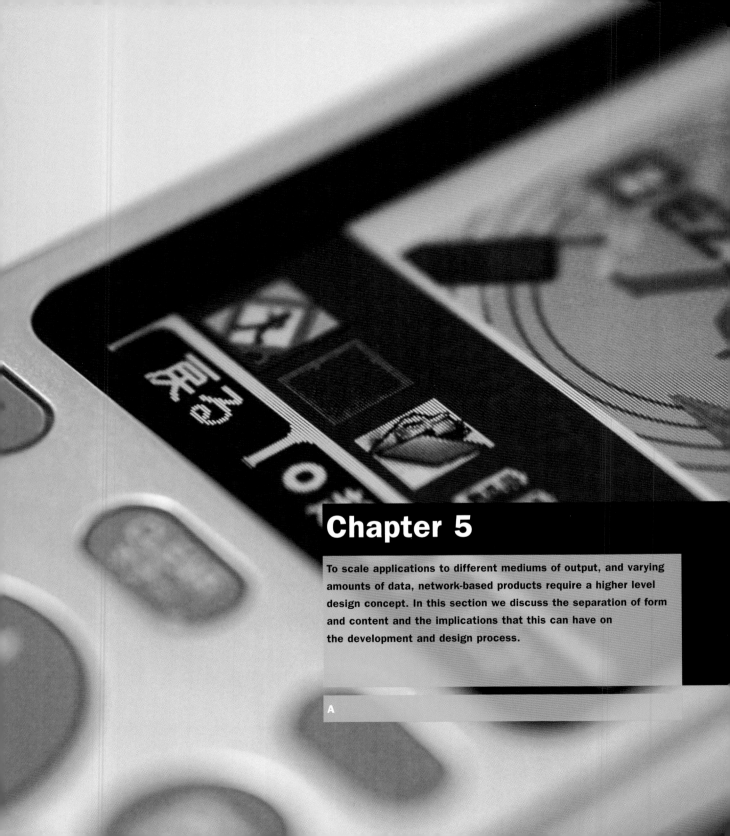

Chapter 5

To scale applications to different mediums of output, and varying amounts of data, network-based products require a higher level design concept. In this section we discuss the separation of form and content and the implications that this can have on the development and design process.

A

The Network on Small Screens

Here we look at the new services that are emerging for small-screen devices, among which location-based services seem to be the most appropriate for the medium. Coupled with this, traditional entertainment media such as radio or television are developing programmes that are suitable for small-screen display.

This section offers a glossary of terms to help decode network lingo. Acronyms from XML to UMTS and the major milestones of the telecommunication roadmap are explained.

B

C

Most of the content that is displayed on small screens is not composed of local data; more and more information is instead called up via a network when it is needed. This increases the challenge for the designer, who must increasingly consider usage scenarios and functionality as well as create space for them in the navigation structure and on the display. The designer is no longer dealing with the specific information design, but instead has to develop the rules by which the content is presented on the screen. This means that all concepts must be scalable; they must work equally well with large and small quantities of data.

A community where the user represents themselves with virtual identities (or avatars), works well if it consists of 3–20 persons. However, if it consists of a larger number of users then, this form of access can no longer be presented successfully.

Lists, extendable menus or forms that only show a fragment of the content – because the designer did not anticipate that the content entered might be longer than the space that was permitted – are far from ideal. A possible solution for this problem is the incorporation of functionality that allows dynamic changes to the text size.

The automatic rendering of scroll bars to navigate the screen is not an elegant design solution, simply because they will not always be necessary.

The presentation of all of the shopping sites on the world wide web as a virtual high street only works to a limited extent because there are just too many options, so the street would be infinitely long. By limiting the search criteria the range of options can be concentrated so that a pictorial metaphor will work.

Metaphors

Metaphors, which are often used in virtual communities, are especially difficult to scale. The more specific the reference to reality, the more difficult it is to maintain an overview of a growing volume of data. The advantage of intuitive access is lost because of the lack of clarity.

Databases

Most electronic information is stored in databases, retrieved dynamically and incorporated into the layout. In many cases the database structure is either fixed, or the data are drawn from existing databases. To design the optimum concept for use and an attractive and intuitive visual software interface, the designer should find out as much as possible in the concept development phase about the information that can be retrieved from the database and the structure within which it is stored and linked.

The existing database structure is the predominant factor that determines how easily a user can access and organise the desired information.

1a

PHONE BOOK

Emma home
TEL: 123456-7
FAX: 123456-8
Emma office
TEL: 7654321
FAX:
Emma mobile
TEL: 0175-1234567
FAX:

1b

ADDRESSES

ID	FIRST NAME	SURNAME	TEL	FAX	E-MAIL	STREET	POST CODE	TOWN
01								
02	Emma home	Muster	123456-7	123456-8	em@gmx.com	Elmstreet 7	10000	Berlin
03	Emma office		7654321		muster@seven5.com			
04	Emma mobile		0175-1234567					

2a

PHONE BOOK

Emma
home: 123456-7
office: 7654321
mobile: 0175-1234567
fax: 123456-8

2b

ADDRESSES

ID	FIRST NAME	SURNAME	STREET	POST CODE	TOWN
01					
02	Emma	Muster	Elmstreet 7	10000	
03					
04					

ID MAIL 02

	private	office	family	other
em@gmx.com	×			
muster@seven5.com		×		
emma@gmx.com				×
emma@muster.com			×	

ID PHONE 02

	home	office	mobile	fax	pager	other
123456-7	×					
0175-1234567			×			
123456-8				×		
7654321		×				

The **structure of the database** determines how convenient it is to use. If it does not offer enough fields to save all of the required information, (as in example 1a), the user will have to improvise and create a second record for the same purpose.

A convenient user interface in which the user can add any number of entries to a single record requires a careful design of the underlying database structure (as in example 2b). Here, the designer is responsible for acting on behalf of the user and advocating this solution, even though it requires a greater amount of programming work.

Creative alternative categories, such as searches for an alternative travel destination with the same temperature or journey time as a previously searched destination, requires additional tables in the database, which are linked via these alternative categories of information.

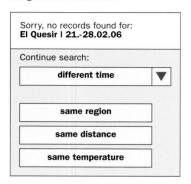

Keeping with the travel theme, when making **bookings**, the user often has to input exact journey details and is then given a negative response because the system fails to find an exact data match. It is a better solution if the system allowed the user to define a frame within which they wish to travel, because this would increase the number of results.

If the project is on a larger scale, and a new database structure is developed specifically for an application, the designer must be actively involved from the outset. In their role as the user's advocate, the designer should anticipate and develop all the possible scenarios for use, and create a list of requirements for the underlying organisational structure of the data. If this is not done there is a risk that the designer will merely be able to compound inconsistent or complicated user dialogues by means of the form and design.

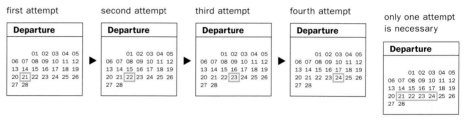

Different output media

The networking of different computer platforms presents another challenge to the designer, as many applications are published at the same time on different output media. The designer must ensure that the application is implemented in an appropriate way for the output medium, and is still recognisable across different media. Differences in the screen format, display quality and form of interaction have to be taken into account – sometimes using the same colour scheme might be the only link between two different output media.

Depending on the device and application in question, the designer may need to develop different output masks that are geared to each medium. In some cases, such as the special browsers for smart phones, the browser implements the HTML code specifically for this screen size, but in other cases, special HTML pages must be created in order to achieve the best possible display. In each case, the designer must analyse the usage concept and then define the volume of the content and the available options for each output device.

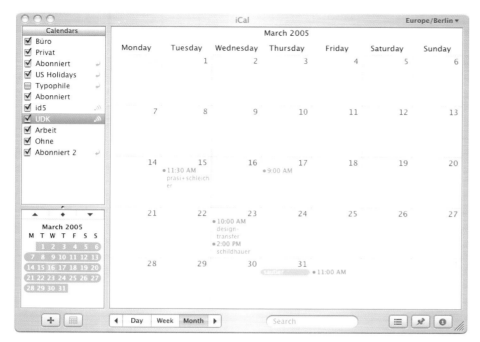

Where the same content is displayed and manipulated **on a PC and on a small portable device**, recognition is an important factor. Although the configuration, range of functions and the form of interaction are different, the design should create a formal similarity in order to reduce the amount of time the user requires to adapt to the new interface.

If the software comes from two different manufacturers, in this case iCal from Apple (left), and a calendar from Sony Ericsson (above), this is likely to impair the consistency of the display.

This **separation of form and content** means that the designer must develop an abstract design grid, generalise their design resources and develop usage rules. In practice, this means that the interface tends to become visually poor and monotonous because defining rules that can always be applied is a far more complex affair than defining stand-alone individual solutions. Yet at the same time, the challenge for the designer is to be far more systematic and functional in the way that they work. Generally, this helps to make the user guidance consistent, so that the user is not faced with any surprises, but in individual cases it can also make the navigation logic more complicated because it is impossible to provide customised solutions.

Advanced design exercise
Adapt a familiar website for a small-screen device. What would Amazon or eBay look like on a smaller screen? How can the characteristics of a brand and its website be preserved, but at the same time creatively adapted to suit the changed conditions of the screen size and form of interaction?

Small mobile devices can offer a **wide range of informative and entertaining functions**. Initially, classic formats were adapted from other media forms, such as radio or television. To make such applications easy to handle, it is now common for the interface to borrow control elements from the old medium.

Universal Remote Control irRemote (Psiloc): the realistic rendering of a physical remote control enables the user to operate the software easily.

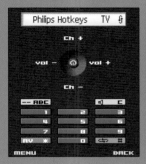

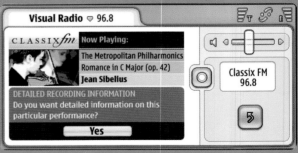

Visual Radio (Nokia 3230, Nokia 7710): can now transmit information about the music that is being played (such as the name of the artist) or the commercial advertising (such as where to buy the recording) at the same time as supplying the audio function.

Supplementing the main medium of the radio by a visual, interactive platform allows rapid access to background information and direct participation from the listener.

More and more products in our environment are networked and have their own address on the internet. This means that the personal, mobile and networked product becomes a remote control which can be used to check-in with other devices, for example those in the home.

Network operator → → → → **Internet**

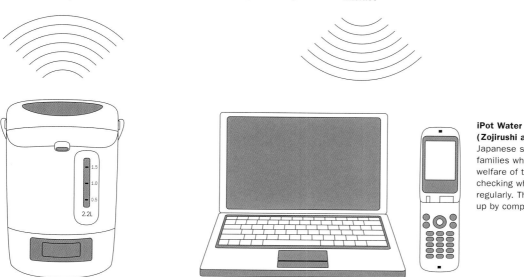

iPot Water Jug with an Internet Address (Zojirushi and NTT DoCoMo): this Japanese service appeals to those families who want to keep an eye on the welfare of their elderly relatives by checking whether the water jug is used regularly. This information can be called up by computer or mobile phone.

TV Wristwatch NHJ VTV-101: this device is a mini TV with a 1.5 inch TFT screen that has 280x220 pixels. Images that are suitable for small-screen devices require special editing, for example more close-ups, but a standardised television programme does not currently take this into account.

30 mm x 23.5 mm

Smart Watches/MSN Direct: this watch offers various service channels, such as the weather forecast or stock market news. The screen's monochrome display and the low resolution is reminiscent of first generation mobile phones.

The creation of new **service ideas for mobile use** is still very much in its infancy. The fact that a personal mobile device will know where it is and what the preferences, habits and needs of its owner are, will necessitate the development of a whole range of new applications. Once realised, the small screen will act as a digital information level that is brought into line with the analogue situation which the user is in. An important role of the designer is to continually identify the needs of users and to develop scenarios for appropriate service concepts.

Postcards by Shutterfly™: this is a mobile photographic laboratory and postal service provided by Shutterfly; an internet photo services company. Digital pictures can be taken and sent directly as electronic postcards.

lastminute.com: offers 'on the road' travel services. This has long been available on the internet, but is a sensible application for mobile small-screen devices too. The challenge on the comparatively small display is to present a map that is easy to understand.

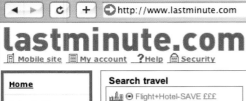

34 mm x 45 mm

Naviwalk (au by KDDI): this navigation aid is designed for mobile use. The digital divining rod helps the user to locate addresses or to arrange meetings. Due to the high resolution, the map display is relatively detailed. (240 x 320 pixels)

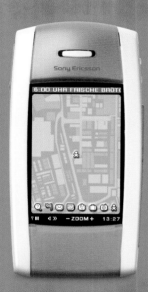

42 mm x 64 mm

My Companion: this is a concept for a personal navigation system. The search criteria are based on the current needs of the user, such as 'I am hungry'. The context has reduced colour display to emphasise the markings on the map. (Katharina Schlosser, 2002, 208 x 320 pixels)

56.4 mm x 56.4 mm

Mobile Multimedia Guide CARLISLE (Lapavalley): this digital guide allows the user to call up historical data about their location. During the course of a real walk through the town of Carlisle, a user can add digital information about the location. (320 x 320 pixels)

Glossary

Bandwidth describes the amount of information that a communication channel can carry. Analogue bandwidth is measured in hertz (Hz), cycles per second. Digital bandwidth (bps or b/s) is measured in bits per second. High bandwidth data connections permit internet users to download files rapidly and to view high-quality, real-time video.

Bluetooth is an open specification for seamless short-range wireless data and voice communications between mobile and stationary devices. For instance, it specifies how mobile phones, computers and PDAs interconnect with each other, with computers, and with office or home phones. The first generation of Bluetooth permits the exchange of data up to a rate of 1 Mbps, even in areas with a great deal of electromagnetic disturbance. Bluetooth transmits and receives via a short-range radio link using a globally available frequency band (4.4 GHz ISM band).

Broadband refers to a high bandwidth communications link, usually over the internet.

Browser: this is a program or 'viewer' that allows Internet users to access pages on the world wide web.

GPS: the Global Positioning System consists of a series of 24 geosynchronous satellites that continuously transmit their position to facilitate terrestrial location detection. They are accurate to between 10–100 meters, depending on the device. They are used in personal tracking, navigation and automatic vehicle location systems.

i-Mode is a packet-based wireless service launched by NTT DoCoMo. It operates at 9.6 Kbps, uses a subset of HTML and is very popular for e-mail and the transfer of icons.

Infrared is a band of the electromagnetic spectrum usually used for short range (up to 20 feet), and air-based data transmission. Data are transmitted from point to point by infrared light, which requires a line of sight between two devices. The IrDA (Infrared Data Association) sets standards for using infrared transmission to ensure that communications between different computers, PDAs, printers, digital cameras, remote controls, etc. are all compatible with one another.

Java is a programming language that is specifically designed to write programs, which can be safely downloaded from the internet and immediately run without fear of viruses. Web pages that use small Java programs (called 'Applets') can include functions such as animations or calculators.

Mbps, Mb/s or Mbit/s: abbreviations of Megabits per second. A measure of data transfer speed on networks (one megabit equals one million bits).

MBps or MB/s refers to MegaBytes per second, which is the unit of measurement for data transfer speed for interfaces like USB.

Roaming is the means by which a mobile phone links up to different base stations as they come within range. International roaming means that a customer can make use of other networks when abroad. Some networks offer different charges and facilities for users travelling abroad.

WAP: Wireless Application Protocol is a secure specification that allows users to access information via hand-held wireless devices.

Wi-Fi is short for 'wireless fidelity'. The Wi-Fi Alliance seeks to promote wireless networking arrangements based on the IEEE 802.11 specification. Products approved by the Alliance receive the Wi-Fi certified seal of interoperability. The maximum range is anything up to about 100 meters.

WLAN: a Wireless Local Area Network that uses high frequency radio signals to transmit and receive data over distances of a few hundred feet.

XML: eXtensible Mark-up Language, is a pared-down version of the Standard Generalised Mark-Up Language (SGML), designed especially for Web documents. It allows designers to create their own customised tags, enabling the definition, transmission, validation, and interpretation of data between applications and between organisations.

The generations of mobile communications

1G: the first generation of systems for mobile telephones was analogue, circuit switched and only carried voice traffic using frequencies around 900 MHz. The analogue phones used in 1G were less secure and more prone to interference when the signal was weak. Analogue systems include AMPS, NMT and ETACS.

2G: second-generation protocols use digital encoding and include GSM, D-AMPS (TDMA) and CDMA. These protocols support high-bit rate voice communication and limited data communication. They offer auxiliary services such as data transfer, fax, SMS and WAP internet access. Most 2G protocols offer different levels of encryption.

2.5G protocols extend 2G systems to provide additional features such as packet-switched connection (GPRS) and enhanced data rates (HSCSD, EDGE). 2.5G is the most significant step towards 3G, as it requires similar business models and service and network architecture.

3G: third-generation protocols support much higher data rates, and are intended for advanced applications. 3G is known as IMT-2000 (International Mobile Telecommunications-2000) by the ITU and is commonly implemented as UMTS, and as CDMA2000 in North America.

UMTS: the Universal Mobile Telecommunications System is a mobile communications system that offers direct connection between terminals and satellites. UMTS will facilitate the delivery of new services and capabilities in low-cost, high-capacity mobile communications, with data rates of up to 2 Mbps and worldwide roaming.

3.5G is an improvement of the third generation systems that benefits from the HSDPA-enabled W-CDMA infrastructure.

HSDPA: High Speed Downlink Packet Access is a packet-based data service feature of the WCDMA standard, which provides a downlink with data transmission up to 8–10 Mbps.

WCDMA: Wideband Code Division Multiple Access is one of two 3G standards that uses a wider spectrum than CDMA, and can therefore transmit and receive information faster and more efficiently.

4G: fourth generation WWAN communications systems are characterised by high-speed data rates of 20+ Mbps, suitable for high-resolution video and television. Initial deployments are anticipated in 2006–2010.

WWAN: the Wireless Wide Area Network uses common carrier-provided lines.

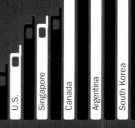

Internet compatibility of mobile phones in % (2003)

Source: Ministry of Public Management, Home Affairs, Posts and Telecommunications, Japan

U.S. | Singapore | Canada | Argentina | South Korea

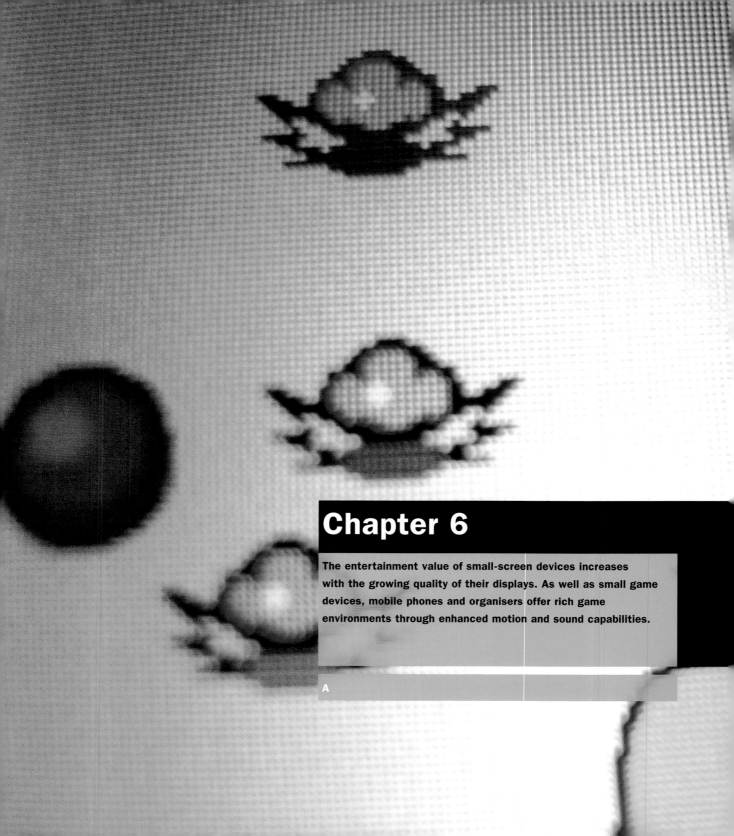

Chapter 6

The entertainment value of small-screen devices increases
with the growing quality of their displays. As well as small game
devices, mobile phones and organisers offer rich game
environments through enhanced motion and sound capabilities.

A

Entertainment on Small Screens

Here we look at applications such as miniature photo-editing, and explore the possibility that their added entertainment value could soon provide just as much fun as the small-screen versions of established computer games.

In this section we offer a classification model for games of any kind. We also look at the market share of entertaining applications in different regions around the world.

B

C

Nowadays, most people own a small, portable device of some sort and, equally, most tend to carry their device with them at all times. Except for pure game consoles, these devices contain confidential personal information and are individually configured by the user. The supplementary entertainment value of the devices has increased with the growing quality of the display, the wealth of new digital services available and increasing transmission speeds. Animated icons, background graphics, polyphonic ring tones and music clips also offer a wealth of bespoke options that are intensively and consistently used, particularly by young target groups. Additionally, games that can be downloaded on to the device or played online are becoming increasingly popular.

Entertainment value

Since the invention of graphical user interfaces there has been a fundamental rule for design: no interface shall be without an entertainment value of some description. This especially applies to the design of small-screen devices because they are far more personal than a personal computer. The resolution of the screens that are used will soon be a negligible constraint, but the limitations of physical size will remain an important parameter. Nevertheless, small-screen devices can develop a range of entertainment values.

Games

Games are the high-art form of interaction design, as well as an arena for the experimental exploration of new forms of interaction, because the user's participation in a game is always optional. If the game is not fun, or if the way it works is too complex, it will not be used. Many interaction components have developed from control features in games, such as the joystick.

The logic of games

Games on small, portable devices are often used to simply pass the time en route. The user should understand the concept of the game immediately so that play can commence without delay. This is why traditional or classic games are often adapted for the small screen; they work at once because they are already familiar. The forms of interaction within the game however, must be adapted to the possibilities of the device. The mini joystick, which is present on most devices, is a relatively powerful input element. The integration of position and acceleration sensors into small-screen devices enables new physical games to be developed.

Moving image

In animation clips or video extracts, the size and proportions of the display will determine the choice of motif and the extract shown. Complex scenarios and camera-panning techniques in which the focus of the action is difficult to follow should be avoided. The contrast between dynamic and static image elements is the main design feature that should be incorporated on small-screen devices. Focal ranges such as close-ups or long shots work best on the small screen, either to convey detail (such as facial expressions), or to give an overview of the situation. The fact that the context in which small screens are used is so varied means that differences in colour and brightness may need to be exaggerated to ensure that the whole sequence will work in daylight.

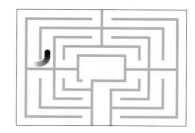

On small-screen devices using **motion** to attract the user's eye is a powerful technique.

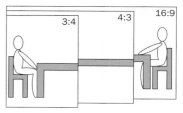

Most small-screen devices have a portrait **screen format**. This might contradict our viewing habits for moving pictures, so the designer may need to rethink the selection of the extract shown.

Long shots or **close-ups** work best on small screens. With middle zoom levels, the user is unable to see the detail or the context.

Sound

Sound is a significant entertainment factor that can make the handling of a device easier and more enjoyable by providing positive support for the user's interactions. When sound is used in games, it can be annoying if it is constantly repeated without any variation, but as the storage space of devices increases, more subtle and varied sound effects can be created and incorporated. However, peripheral use of devices in public places can restrict the use of sound, therefore good games should work equally well without sound, otherwise the user may be dependent on using headphones.

For audio devices, headphones make the sound a very personal and intense experience for the user. They help the listener to focus as they prevent any surrounding acoustic interruption. Unlike image, here the size of the output device is of no relevance.

Many first generation digital games, such as Pacman or Tetris, have survived in their original basic format, and they only need to be adapted to accommodate the latest technical standards. See also Section B in this chapter.

Advanced design exercise

Adapt the game of chess so that it is suitable for a small screen of 240 x 320 pixels with 262,000 available colours. Design clearly distinguishable chess pieces, and consider the manner of interaction via use of soft keys and a mini joystick.

The desire for **individual and enhanced forms of expression** continues to stimulate the development of entertainment applications. The small screen has long been established as an independent medium and the art of being creative with limited resources in a small space has led to a variety of expression and forms a whole new type of aesthetics.

ASCII Art: pictures can be generated by using text symbols. ASCII art uses the screen as a canvas and applies the text input of the mobile phone in surprisingly creative ways.

Deco Mail (NTT DoCoMo 900i Series): with rich text massages a variety of creative messaging designs are possible for mobile phones that have an e-mail function. Apart from a choice of fonts and colours, it is also possible to integrate graphics and other files in the message.

www.micromovie-award.com: feature films in pocket format are becoming a new art form. The available screen space and the volume of data required to play the movie present a creative challenge for the designer.

Photographic Post-Processing Software is becoming an increasingly popular addition to mobile phones. Individual images can be generated, or ready-made graphic elements can combine the processed images into comic strips.

Kirari Mail (Panasonic P252iS): the user can select a coloured light strip to tell others what mood he is in.

Donkey Kong Junior (Nintendo Game & Watch, 1982, 5.3 x 3.5 mm)

53 mm x 35 mm

From the launch of the early gaming consoles, efforts have been made to ensure that small-screen devices are considered as **complete entertainment machines**. The simple games that were available on first generation devices such as Donkey Kong and Tetris are now supplied with almost every mobile phone, or can be downloaded from the network on to a multitude of devices. Internet-based multi-player games, which are mainly played on desktop computers at the moment, are likely to become a popular leisure activity on mobile devices in the foreseeable future too.

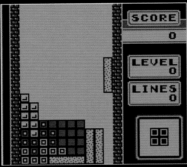

Original Tetris for Game Boy Classic (160 x 144 pixels, 83 dpi, monochrome, four brightness levels)

Tetris for pocket PC (240 x 320 pixels 114 dpi)

3D-Tetris for Palm (320 x 320 pixels, 147 dpi)

Tetris for Nokia 3200 (128 x 128 pixels, 119 dpi, 4,096 colours)

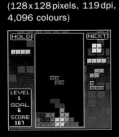

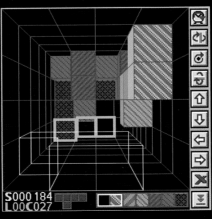

Wario Ware Twisted (Nintendo 2005):
The use of position sensors means that
new forms of interaction are now
possible. The interaction on the screen
can be controlled by tilting the device.
(240 x 160 pixels)

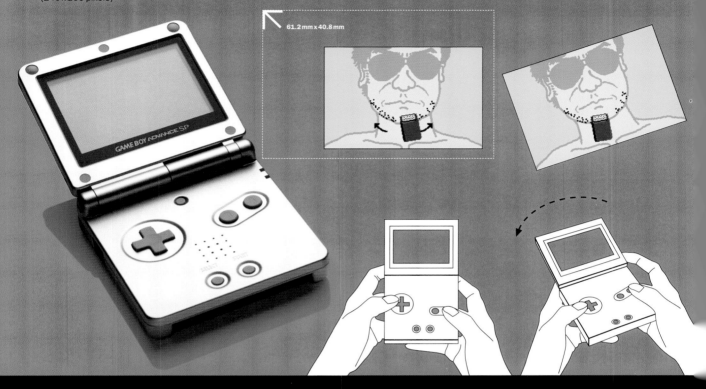

61.2 mm x 40.8 mm

Pacman for pocket PC (240 x 320 pixels, 114 dpi)

**Aqman Challenge for Nokia
3230** (176 x 208 pixels,
130 dpi, 65,536 colours)

Pacman for Nokia 3100
(128 x 128 pixels, 119 dpi,
4,096 colours)

Pacman for Nokia 3410
(96 x 65 pixels, 81 dpi,
monochrome)

Playing games is part of the human nature; many games that are played today are hundreds of years old. Games of chance using dice, for example, have existed for almost 3,000 years.

Our motivation is to challenge destiny, compete with other players or improve our own performance. Most classical games have been adapted for digital media and are now also available in a suitable format for small screens.

A consistent **classification system** for all games is difficult because most games are a unique mixture of different components and categories. The main parameters to classify games are the factors of **chance, skill, strategy and time**.

Inventing a new game that works is not easy. Classical gaming patterns, such as jump and run, are often reworked. They are given a different narrative framework, and a new and original interaction is created for the game. Role-playing and simulation are game patterns that are based on a carefully constructed narrative framework.

Classic games are now very popular in digital format, for example, **dice games** are largely based on chance, and **chess** is a classic game of strategy. **Darts** is a pure game of skill, but **car racing** is a time-critical game of skill. **Poker** combines the factors of both chance and strategy.

The success of **Tetris** is perhaps due to the fact that all four factors play a role – it is a time-critical game that also combines the factors of chance, skill and strategy. Equally **Super Mario** is a time-critical jump-and-run game that combines chance and skill.

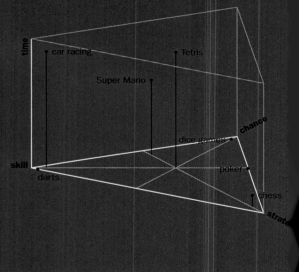

The categories below are very well established, although they are somewhat overlapping and inconsistent. Many of the game developers reject existing and established categories and prefer to declare their newly developed game to be in a class of its own.

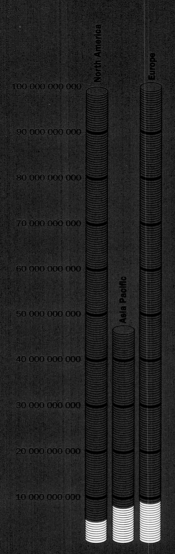

North America
Europe
Asia Pacific

100 000 000 000

90 000 000 000

80 000 000 000

70 000 000 000

60 000 000 000

50 000 000 000

40 000 000 000

30 000 000 000

20 000 000 000

10 000 000 000

Youth spending on mobile products in EUR, in proportion to total spending 2006.

Source: mobileYouth – w2forum.com

download

online

Proportional market share of downloadable games and online games 2005.

Source: Global Information Inc. (GII)

racing

role-play

shooter

simulation

sports

strategy

Chapter 7

In the first part of this chapter we explore the art of typography and how it can be translated to the digital domain in general, and to the small screen in particular. We examine ways to enhance readability and focus on the dynamic representation of text and text input. Finally we discuss the design of icons, taking into account parameters such as icon size, interaction style and specific icon features.

A

Digital Hieroglyphs:
Text and Icons on Small Screens

In the second section of the chapter we look at different examples of typography on small-screen displays. We review the additional items of screen content, such as pictures and movies, which text and icons need to complement. In addition, we present a collection of icons that serve to demonstrate the variety and potential of visual communication.

B

In this section we show a selection of typefaces and font sizes that are suited for use on the small screen. We also explain the techniques of antialiasing and ClearType and finally, deliver a short glossary of some of the typographical terms that are relevant for small screens.

C

Text is the visual interface for language. In contrast to speech, which is linear and will usually need to be heard in full before the listener can understand the meaning, written text offers a variety of possibilities for access and use. Written text can be read thoroughly, skimmed through or it can be 'scanned' for keywords or phrases. Although small-screen devices are already multimedia machines, the incorporation of text on the display will play a decisive role as an information medium. This is probably because the transmission of information by the written word, particularly in a public setting, can be done far more discreetly than by the spoken word.

Text

The presentation of text on small-screen devices is a special challenge for the designer, and the primary motive must be to ensure legibility. The most significant factor that affects legibility is the environment that the device will be used in most frequently, for example, will the lighting conditions be ambient or will the user be in a position to concentrate fully on the screen? Fundamentally, the designer must develop a concept that works in the worst possible conditions, such as direct daylight and peripheral use, to ensure that the device will be 'useable' all of the time.

The default text/background **screen contrast** is to position light-coloured type on a dark background. The opposite contrast should only be used if paper is being simulated, for example, in desktop-publishing programs.

The most important **contrast** level on screen-based media is the brightness contrast. Small-screen devices today are not yet sufficiently light-intensive to be clearly legible under direct sunlight, yet the maximum contrast level that will achieve optimum legibility under direct sunlight, is blinding when used under subdued lighting conditions. Some devices, such as navigation systems, are already able to adapt their display to the changing light conditions by offering a day mode and a night mode. This allows a more finely differentiated design and a greater density of detail in the information displayed. In the future we are likely to see devices that have built-in brightness sensors, which have the ability to make similar adjustments smoothly and automatically.

The smaller the type, the greater the selected contrast values should be. The **brightness-contrast value** should not fall below 50% for black-and-white text.

The brightness contrast must be greater for the display of text on small screens than for desktop applications. Whereas a brightness contrast of 30% is clearly legible on larger screens, the contrast values on smaller screens should be at least 50% in order to ensure good legibility in all situations.

50% brightness contrast   30% brightness contrast

Complex or intricate screen backgrounds that do not offer a sufficient constant contrast to the text displayed in the foreground should be avoided in the design and development process. If this is unavoidable, in the case of control functions on camera displays for example, either an extremely rare signal colour can be used, or the type should have a contrasting outline to ensure permanent legibility.

An intricate **background** always makes legibility difficult. It should especially be avoided on small-screen devices.

The **resolution** of small screens is now considerably higher than the resolution of most desktop monitors. Unfortunately, this relatively high resolution is not yet supported by the operating systems of all devices. This means that graphics and icons are presented very clearly, but type still has clearly visible ragged edges when displayed. The varied resolution values of small-screen devices means that the points size or pixel count can only be used as a rough guide to the actual type size rendered on screen. As such it is important to carry out careful research into the technical specifications of the device and take these into account when selecting the type and type size to be displayed.

Small Screens
72 dpi – 16 pt

Small Screens
100 dpi – 11.5 pt

Small Screens
120 dpi – 9.6 pt

Small Screens
144 dpi – 8 pt

Small Screens
200 dpi – 5.7 pt

Type with an upper case height of **16 pixels** can be displayed at very different sizes depending on the resolution of the screen.

If colours are incorporated in the text design, the differences between the intrinsic brightness of each colour used must also be taken into account to ensure the best possible legibility. See also Chapter 8: Layout and Colour on Small Screens.

The selection of **fonts and type sizes** for small-screen devices is subject to the same rules that are applied to all screen applications: the smaller the text, the more the font should be adapted to the special features of the screens. For large headlines or decorative textual elements, it may be possible to incorporate fonts with strongly modulated line widths, such as serif typefaces. However, for body text, a geometrically-regular font that has an even line thickness, orthogonal lines and small radii should be used instead. The relatively narrow column width for text on small screens must also be taken into account, this means that a narrow font should be chosen for body text so that as many words as possible can be fitted on a line and reading can therefore flow comfortably.

For very small text, such as the text on navigation elements and menus, a font that is specifically developed for the screen should be used. The likelihood that hand-held mobile devices will be used peripherally should also be taken into account when selecting the type; all interaction instructions should be easy to understand and succinct. Both the typographical design and the type size must support this, and the text should be displayed as clear, large and visible as possible.

The more detailed a font is, the more pixels it requires for **adequate display**. The strongly modulated characters of Garamond cannot be displayed at a height of six pixels; it requires at least 20 pixels for adequate rendering. In comparison, transfer is optimised to a character height of six pixels.

Small > Small Small

The use of halftone pixels to visually smooth the edges of a character is called **antialiasing**. This technique was developed to better display non-orthogonal lines on the screen. However, as a rule of thumb this technique should not be applied to type that is smaller than 12 pt (with current screen resolutions), as the text will be blurred and difficult to read on screen. The size below which antialiasing should be avoided will vary slightly for each font or type style, and should be checked experimentally on the output device.

This example shows the difference in display of text with (shown on the bottom row), and without (shown on the top row), antialiasing.

The legible presentation of text on the small screen necessitates careful adjustment of the **letter spacing, word spacing and line spacing**. As a rule, letter and word spacing should be increased if antialiasing is used in order to prevent the letters from sticking together. However, it is important to maintain a careful balance between the separation of individual words and the number of words that can be fitted on to a line. The line-spacing value on screen must be increased by at least 10% compared with the value on paper in order to ensure easy legibility.

Increasing the **letter spacing** improves the legibility of text on the screen.

Some **highlighting methods** are very suited to use on the small screen to indicate headings, links or instructions; others though are less suitable.

The use of an italic type style is generally unsuitable for screen display because the slanting strokes of the characters collide with the orthogonal pixel grid of the screen, which makes the type display very irregular.

Highlighting methods: bold, italic or coloured lettering, and coloured backgrounds, can help distinguish different textual elements.

The use of bold type is suitable for highlighting text as long as the letter spacing is sufficient enough to ensure that the characters do not run into each other.

The use of colour is also a suitable highlighter, but to a limited extent; partly because the low number of colours makes colour detection more difficult and partly because no other colour combination can achieve the same brightness contrast as black and white. However, if the main body text has a slightly reduced contrast, such as the use of grey text on a white or black background, the opposite colour (black or white) can then be used for highlighting with the maximum contrast value. Another suitable technique is to position highlighted text on to a colour background. This technique allows the colour to be recognised because the surface is large enough. However, the intrinsic brightness of the colour must be taken into account, and the highlighted text must be inverted if necessary.

The **highlighted text** examples on the right demonstrate the better alternatives for the screen.

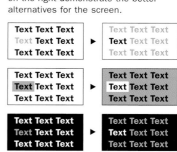

Interaction with small screens is typically characterised by greater user impatience and shorter reading times or attention spans than with large screens. The interaction scenario must take this into account by displaying legible text in small and easily manageable portions only. See also Chapter 3: Physical Interaction.

Automatic **vertical** scrolling.

The positioning of text on the screen should not be envisaged as a static layout, because the process of reading can be regarded as dynamic. As such **dynamic text display** is a viable design option; this means that text can be displayed in a 'flowing' movement to resemble the reading process. Essentially the device automatically scrolls the display at reading speed; examples of this are horizontal, single-line moving text displays such as a news ticker on the television, or vertical scrolling of whole text passages.

If horizontal single-line scrolling is incorporated, care must be taken to ensure that the screen proportions and type size enable a minimum number of words to be visible at the same time, otherwise it is difficult for the user to grasp the content. Ideally, the user should be able to control the speed of the text flow too. Horizontal single-line scrolling technology is most suitable for short sentences and slogans.

Automatic vertical scrolling of text passages can help to make longer texts easier to read, as long as the user can adjust the scrolling speed to their preferred individual reading speed or easily stop the flow of text. Vertical text scrolling helps to preserve the mnemonic quality of written text – passages can be located with ease because the characteristic line breaks are not changed.

Another technique that can be effective is alternating the display style of different types of content. This can be used to present more information, especially content in lists, without reducing the type size.

Automatic **horizontal** single-line text scrolling.

Alternating display, for different types of content.

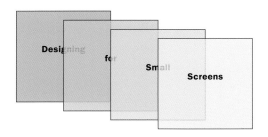

To make it easier to read type on small screens, there are a variety of **text zoom techniques** available that allow single lines or a whole passage of text to be enlarged. A disadvantage of zooming is that if the text runs across the whole screen in a single column, the type size must be changed to display the text in magnified form, and doing so will alter the line breaks. Depending on the zoom factor and the screen size, this can lead to a very disjointed text display.

A solution to this is the use of semantic zoom. This technique reconfigures the text according to the zoom factor used. If there is not enough available space, only a few keywords are shown, but the content is shown in more detail if space permits.

If there is not much space, only a few keywords are displayed, but if there is more space available the content is shown in more detail.

Not much space, a few keywords. More space, content in more detail.

Space, content, keywords.

Semantic zoom: the text content is displayed in direct proportion to the available screen space.

Text input by the user can be regarded as the greatest challenge for small mobile devices. The problem has less to do with the screen itself and more an issue of physical interaction, which may differ considerably from familiar text input techniques (such as via a keyboard), depending on the device.

Graffiti techniques require a special alphabet to be learned in order to enable unambiguous character recognition on a touchscreen, but these techniques are relatively complicated. Multiple characters assigned to single keys (such as those on a mobile phone), is probably the most widespread text-inputting technique for small-screen devices.

Slightly larger devices that incorporate a touchscreen and stylus often have virtual keyboards that appear temporarily on the screen. If the virtual keyboards retain the familiar QWERTY layout, they offer the user a synchronous optical display of all functions; this is the fastest way to enter text on small screens without connecting an external keyboard.

There are many different concepts for one- or two-handed text-input interaction. See also Chapter 3: Physical Interaction.

Graffiti handwriting recognition: used on the Palm OS, this requires a special alphabet, which is then interpreted.

Keys with **multiple character assignment.**

A **virtual keyboard** used in conjunction with a stylus input.

The success of computer-assisted systems would be unthinkable without the use of icons. The 'graphical user interface' (GUI), made the use of computers possible for non-specialists. The desktop metaphor and its associated icons established a recognised standard, which was representative of quite complex information exchanges between the system and the user. Symbolic actions of the user, such as putting something in the dustbin, translates what are actually complex information transactions into understandable concepts, as they are borrowed from real life.

Icons

Using icons on small screens is useful, and justifiably popular. Even if they are not logically connected by a narrative framework, icons still allow fast non-verbal communication between the system and the user. However, designers must develop icons carefully if they are to be commonly understood. For functions that were conceived in the digital arena, such as email, the icons that are used to indicate them will often draw on the established associations of their pre-digital form.

Using the principle of **redundant coding** means that the extra picture caption helps the user to interpret the icon. (Nokia 6310)

For an icon to communicate successfully, the metaphorical image and its meaning in a digital context must be learned first. To ensure this, redundant coding is used: the icon is supported by a textual explanation, which the user can refer to if they are in doubt of the icon's meaning. With use of the device the icon itself will offer enough information for the user to understand. An additional option is to incorporate animated icons; this method can be used to communicate more complicated information and actions.

All stages of abstraction can be used in the design of icons. If the space and the graphical capabilities of the device permit, photographic images or sophisticated illustrations can be used. Equally, the smaller the amount of available space and the more limited a device's colour scheme is, the more archetypical the icons should be.

Icons often incorporate **elaborate design detail**, because of the need to make the interface easily discernable from others; but these details can make the interface harder to understand. Originality in the choice of design and the analogy may backfire if the user does not understand the symbols used.

Icon alphabets work across language barriers; they form the traffic signs of a digital application that the user looks for when they wish to navigate a program. To avoid confusing the user and to achieve visual consistency, all icons within a system should have the same degree of abstraction.

The gap between **common sense and originality** defines the window of opportunity for the design of icons. Depending on the recipient and the application, the metaphorical image used may vary. The designer must take into account whether or not the target group consists of users who are experienced with digital media. The type of user will be a crucial factor in the decision of whether an imaginative metaphor can be used, or if the icon should be more conventional and easy to understand.

For most applications, only the top level of the hierarchy and its corresponding tools are described by icons. If the user then chooses to navigate lower levels of the hierarchy, the additional options are displayed as text descriptions. Icons therefore, are limited in their descriptive capability; once a certain degree of complexity is reached, icons become ambiguous and lose their advantages over text descriptions.

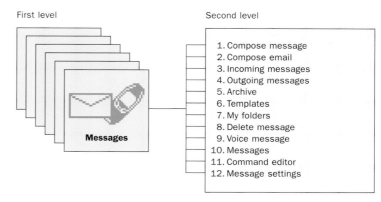

First level

Second level

1. Compose message
2. Compose email
3. Incoming messages
4. Outgoing messages
5. Archive
6. Templates
7. My folders
8. Delete message
9. Voice message
10. Messages
11. Command editor
12. Message settings

Messages

The structure of a device's **navigation levels** will often determine icon use. At the highest level the categories can be represented by icons, but at the secondary level the selection choices are too specific to be unambiguously represented by an icon. (Nokia 6310)

Basic design exercise

Develop an icon that represents the function 'find a restaurant'. This icon should have the capacity to be used at various display sizes and resolutions.

Consider whether an animated icon could help to communicate the content more clearly.

For further examples see Section B in this chapter.

Used as a label on a **row of tabs**, an icon is remembered both by its appearance as well as its location.

In the quest for the optimum use of available space on a small screen, the **size of icons** is a distinct advantage. Icons can offer a great deal of information that simply could not be displayed in text form in the same space. The size of an icon is directly connected to the user's form of interaction with the device, for example, if a stylus is used for input, the element for selection can be displayed at a very small size.

Also, the arrangement of the icons on the screen display supports a user's spatial memory capacity. This means that functions can be found faster because the user remembers both the icon and its position. This applies to the main navigation levels such as those used in many mobile phones and in the navigation and function bars of Pocket PCs.

Stylus-controlled interfaces allow the **smallest icons** to be displayed.

Direct input with a stylus changes the design criteria for icons, as an icon can be selected very accurately. This means that icons can even be displayed at the very small size of 9x9 pixels. For icons of this size to be legible, it is necessary to use: strong contrasts, very simplified forms and no antialiasing. However, colour coding at this size can be used, but only to a limited extent because the space available is just not large enough to distinguish the colours. It would be just about possible to use the two signal colours of red and green because they are distinctive enough even on small spaces.

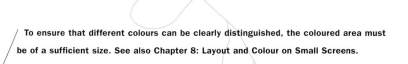

To ensure that different colours can be clearly distinguished, the coloured area must be of a sufficient size. See also Chapter 8: Layout and Colour on Small Screens.

144I145 >

For those devices with **indirect interaction by scroll wheel or jogdial** the icon also serves as a pointer device to tell the user where they are within the system. In order for this to work effectively the icon variations must be visibly changed in its colour, size or contrast to clearly show which option is currently active, and the icon must be allowed sufficient space for this change to be clearly visible. If the change is also to be highlighted by an alteration in size, then the necessary space for the maximum display size must be reserved around the icon. Icons are typically between 16–32 pixels in size.

Each icon must have different **display states** developed: active, inactive and selected, so that the user will know where they are in the system

Direct interaction with a touchscreen is the most space consuming technique. Icons that represent the options on a touchscreen must be large enough to be selected by a fingertip, and this is usually a larger area than an icon would need for visualisation. Displays with touchscreens therefore have a much lower density of addressable interaction elements. Increasingly, to circumvent this limitation, touchscreens work with gesture recognition: the user carries out a metaphorical movement, which the system understands as icon input.

Interactive elements on touchscreens should have a **physical size** of at least 15 x 15 mm, and the distance between the elements should be at least 5 mm.

15 x 15 mm at 72 dpi > 43 x 43 pixels

15 x 15 mm at 110 dpi > 66 x 66 pixels

15 x 15 mm at 144 dpi > 86 x 86 pixels

Alice Pixel Font Family: this font offers eight individually composed letter sizes, ranging from five to 12 pixels. This affords the designer greater scope than conventional pixel fonts, which are usually only available in one size. (Schröder+Wendt, 2005)

Legibility is the most important criterion on small screens. Narrow letter spacing and robust characters are needed due to limited space and insufficient resolution for typographical refinements.

ALICE.MICRO	ABCDEFGHIJKLMNOPQRSTUVWXYZÄÖÜoabcdefghijkLmnopqrstuvwxyzäöüβ0123456789
ALICE.5	ABCDEFGHIJKLMNOPQRSTUVWXYZÄÖÜoabcdefghijkLmnopqrstuvwxyzäöäöüβ012334456
ALICE.6	ABCDEFGHIJKLMNOPQRSTUVWXYZÄÖÜoabcdefghijkLmnopqrstuvwxyzäöäöüβ012334456
ALICE.7	ABCDEFGHIJKLMNOPQRSTUVWXYZÄÖÜoabcdefghijkLmnopqrstuvwxyzäöäöüβ012334456
ALICE.8	ABCDEFGHIJKLMNOPQRSTUVWXYZÄÖÜoabcdefghijkLmnopqrstuvwxyzäöäöüβ012334456
ALICE.9	ABCDEFGHIJKLMNOPQRSTUVWXYZÄÖÜoabcdefghijkLmnopqrstuvwxyzäöäöüβ012334456
ALICE.10	ABCDEFGHIJKLMNOPQRSTUVWXYZÄÖÜoabcdefghijkLmnopqrstuvwxyzäöäöüβ012334456
ALICE.11	ABCDEFGHIJKLMNOPQRSTUVWXYZÄÖÜoabcdefghijkLmnopqrstuvwxyzäöäöüβ012334456
ALICE.12	ABCDEFGHIJKLMNOPQRSTUVWXYZÄÖÜoabcdefghijkLmnopqrstuvwxyzäöäöüβ012334456

The quick brown fox jumps over the Lazy dog.

The quick brown fox jumps over the Lazy dog.
The quick brown fox jumps over the Lazy dog.
The quick brown fox jumps over the Lazy dog.
The quick brown fox jumps over the Lazy dog.
The quick brown fox jumps over the Lazy dog.
The quick brown fox jumps over the Lazy dog.
The quick brown fox jumps over the Lazy dog.
The quick brown fox jumps over the Lazy dog.

91 mm x 122 mm

Electronic Paper: in the foreseeable future digital paper will be used for a wide range of applications. The properties of electronic paper are similar to those of a sheet of paper, but digital paper is essentially a flexible, lightweight, ultra-thin computer display.

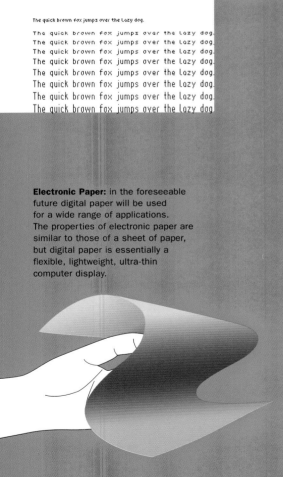

LIBRIé (Sony/Philips): The first device to utilise Philips' E Ink display solution for enhanced reading.

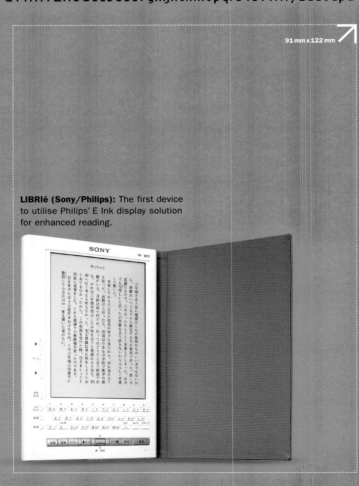

Talby (au by KDDI, 2004): this application offers a scaling function for text display. Text can be displayed at an appropriate size according to the user's eyesight, the light conditions and the context in which the device is used.

Dasher Project: this is a text input program that offers a visual form of word recognition and completion. The user selects individual letters by moving the cursor, and the possibilities for the next letter or word are continuously generated. The user can then select the right option via small cursor movements. At first the system is difficult to get used to, but after some practice it is actually a fairly fast input method. This innovative concept can also be applied to small screens.
(Inference Group Cambridge University: David MacKay, David Ward, 2002)

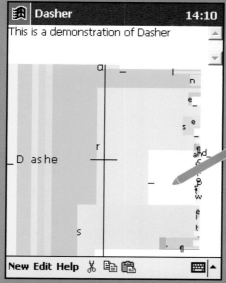

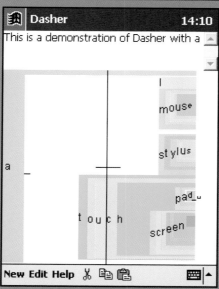

PowerShot Pro 1 (Canon): here, white icons are used to display the camera's setting options. A semi-transparent black background helps to increase the contrast of the icons. Red, Canon's corporate colour, is used to highlight the activated setting.

Cybershot (Sony, 2003): here the settings are permanently displayed. A black surround ensures that the white text does not become blurred, even on a light-coloured background.
If the settings are edited, an opaque surface is added which forms a calm background for the text and icons. The activation colour is yellow: the lightest colour in the chromatic circle. It stands out well from the grey background because of its brightness and saturation.

The advent of colour displays that have increasingly high resolutions, means that it is now possible for the visual appearance of screen interfaces to be clearly distinguished. Here, the **design of icons** plays an important role.

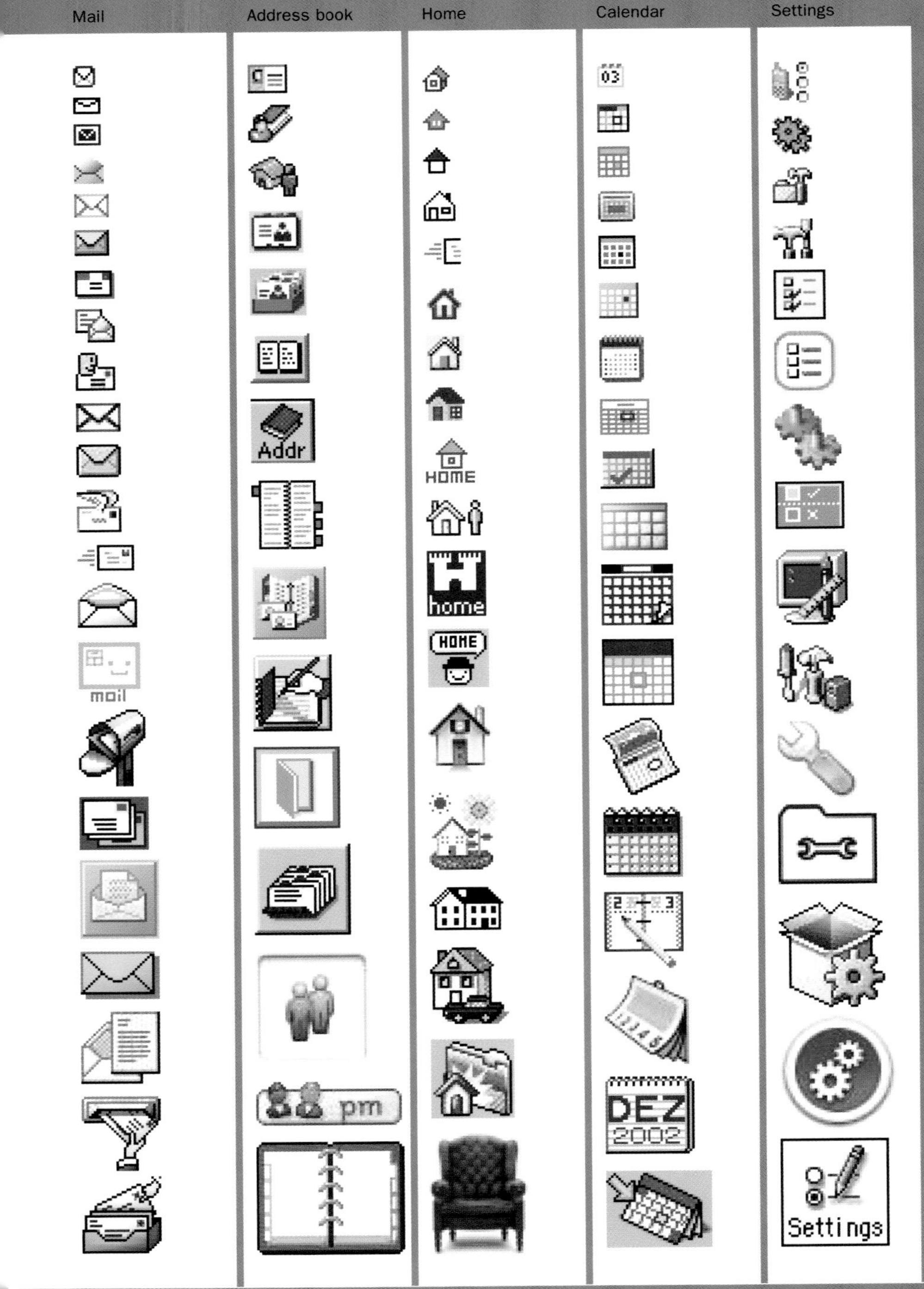

Mail	Address book	Home	Calendar	Settings

V401SA (Vodafone, Sanyo): carefully developed symbols do not need colour to differentiate them or to achieve a high visual quality. As such, colour can instead be used to indicate activation.

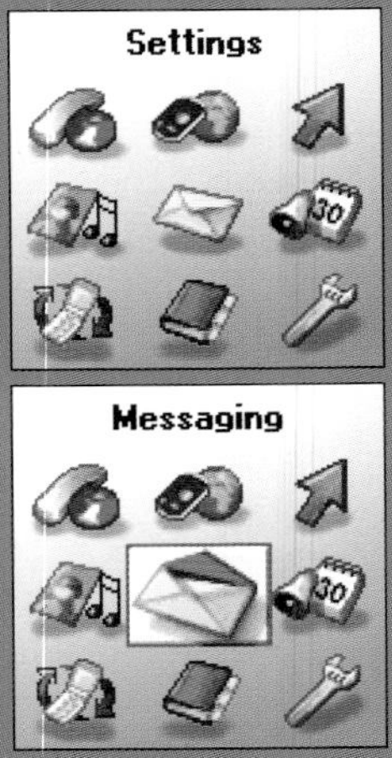

Settings

Messaging

Z200 (Sony Ericsson, 2003): all icons in a software interface should possess the same degree of abstraction and the same visual language. This is not always possible, so the formal link is often created by a three-dimensional presentation style.

Icons should always be developed in at least two states: passive and active. In this example, in addition to a change in the image, the activation is also indicated by a change in size and a frame placed around the icon.

If the available space and resolution quality allows, icons can be designed with a greater degree of detail, which means that they will have an effect on the overall visual appearance. When selecting the icon analogy to use, the experience and background of the target-user group must be taken into account.

Dining: if animated icons are used, even more complex statements are possible. Here the topic of 'dining' is visualised, the function of which proves to be a more time-consuming or leisurely option than simply 'eating'. (Anna Zesewitz, 2003)

Design Exercise in Interface Design: this is an example of the development of an icon by step-by-step abstraction of a photographic illustration. Apart from the selection of a suitable photograph, further corrections are usually necessary to achieve an archetypical image of the object. The smaller the icon to be developed, the fewer individual features the motif can contain. (Zhang Chao, Franziska Langbrandtner, Julia Ellrich, Alexander Gessler, 2004)

Activis Icon Alphabet: the more extensive the alphabet of icons, the simpler and more striking the individual icons should be in their design. An icon should ideally work in black and white; colour can then be used as an extra coding element, for example, to combine icons into groups. (Hendrik Rieß, 2005)

Dynamic Change in Size: with better resolution quality, the icon can also be dynamically scaled, which helps to make selection easier. This principle can also be transferred to the menu selection on small screens. (Dock function, Apple Mac OSX)

Personal electronic communication is a mixed format that is positioned between formal written communication and casual oral communication. The difficulties of text input have favoured the spread of alternative **image-based language forms**. These enable complex content, such as feelings and emotions, to be communicated in just a few simple input actions.

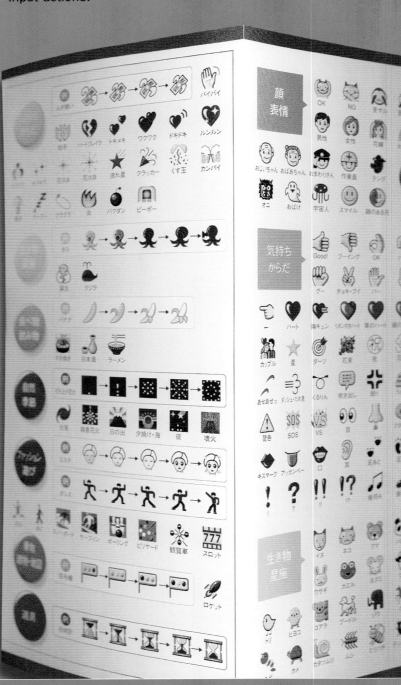

Icons (au by KDDI, 2005): this example shows the variety of icons offered by the Japanese network operator au by KDDI. To provide the user with even more icon options, tips are given on how to combine several icons in order to visualise even more complex content.

The **legibility of a font** on the screen is the designer's most important criterion. The selection of a suitable font should first of all be determined by the display quality on the target screen. The more complex the font, the more pixels it requires.

Type is measured in both **points** (pt) and **pixels** (px), the values of each are only identical when type is displayed at a resolution of 72 dpi. The point size expresses the real height (1 pt = 0.353 mm) of a printed upper case character, but the pixel size will be determined by the pixel size of the output device.

As the resolution of the output device is rarely the same as that of the working medium, it is advisable to use the point size value and to create the document at the same resolution as the output device. This enables the designer to see on the screen how many pixels are available to display a character, and the physical reading size on the output device can be simulated by printing the display.

8 pt	10 pt	12 pt
Arial	Arial	Arial
Comic Sans	Comic Sans	Comic Sans
Courier New	Courier New	Courier New
Georgia	Georgia	Georgia
Impact	Impact	**Impact**
Times New Roman	Times New Roman	Times New Roman
Trebuchet MS	Trebuchet MS	Trebuchet MS
Verdana	Verdana	Verdana
Bodoni	Bodoni F	Bodoni
Franklin Gothic	Franklin Gothic	Franklin Gothic
Frutiger	Frutiger	Frutiger
Futura	Futura	Futura
Garamond	Garamond	Garamond
Helvetica	Helvetica	Helvetica
Lucida Sans	Lucida Sans	Lucida Sans
Officina Sans	Officina Sans	Officina Sans
Palatino	Palatino	Palatino
Rockwell	Rockwell	Rockwell
Tahoma	Tahoma	Tahoma
Univers	Univers	Univers

All fonts at 72 dpi without antialiasing.

72 dpi	110 dpi	144 dpi
12 pt	12 pt	12 pt
12 px	12 px	12 px

The display quality and legibility of most fonts suffer below a font size of 14 pixels, because many typefaces can only be displayed to a limited extent on the pixel grid of the screen. To achieve precise display and good legibility, even with small type sizes, a variety of pixel fonts have been developed that are optimised for a specific number of pixels.

03b (T1) - 5 px
xpaider pixel explosion 01 - 5 px
SILKSCREEN - 5 PX
uni 05_54 - 5 px
BM plain - 5 px
BM mini - 6 px
FuseSeven - 7 px
Unibody 8 - 7 px
VT100 - 7 px
superpoint_rounded - 7 px
superpoint_square - 7 px
Adore64 (T1) - 7 px
AmigaForeverPro - 7 px
Lucida Sans - 8 px
Lucida Sans Typewriter - 8 px
superbly_10_01 - 8 px

8 pt	10 pt	12 pt
Arial	Arial	Arial
Comic Sans	Comic Sans	Comic Sans
Courier New	Courier New	Courier New
Georgia	Georgia	Georgia
Impact	Impact	Impact
Times New Roman	Times New Roman	Times New Roman
Trebuchet MS	Trebuchet MS	Trebuchet MS
Verdana	Verdana	Verdana
Bodoni	Bodoni	Bodoni
Franklin Gothic	Franklin Gothic	Franklin Gothic
Frutiger	Frutiger	Frutiger
Futura	Futura	Futura
Garamond	Garamond	Garamond
Helvetica	Helvetica	Helvetica
Lucida Sans	Lucida Sans	Lucida Sans
Officina Sans	Officina Sans	Officina Sans
Palatino	Palatino	Palatino
Rockwell	Rockwell	Rockwell
Tahoma	Tahoma	Tahoma
Univers	Univers	Univers

All fonts at 72 dpi with antialiasing.

This magnified view shows that the 30° line is at odds with the grid and as such changes from one to two rows of pixels.

The antialiased version of the line on the right has smooth edges.

On the rectangular matrix of the screen, only perfectly horizontal and vertical lines can be drawn precisely. Displaying all other angles and curves will create jagged edges. The technique of antialiasing has been developed to reduce this jagged effect by softening the edges, which visually smoothens the lines. In this technique, the adjoining pixels use colour shades to mediate between the contours and smooth the edges. Type is predestined for antialiasing because the characters frequently change stroke direction, which is usually not in harmony with the pixel matrix. The effect is reversed at type sizes of less than 14 pixels – the type becomes blurred and the characters run into one another.

ClearType technology

This is a new method to improve the display of type edges. Here, the adjoining sub-pixels on the left and the right of an illuminated pixel are addressed, thus achieving a smoothing effect that is similar to antialiasing. However, as Cleartype technology only uses $1/3$ of the width of a full pixel, the resolution by this method is far higher than with conventional antialiasing. ClearType technology does not work if the screen can also be operated in a position swivelled by 90° though.

Without smoothing   Antialiasing   ClearType

Without smoothing   Antialiasing   ClearType

Manually screened

Automatically screened

10x10 pixels

11 x 11 pixels

In the design of icons, **every pixel counts**. To achieve perfect results, icons should be created as bitmap rather than vector file formats. A recognised advantage of vector formats is that they can be scaled, but for an icon this may mean that it is not displayed to its best advantage on the screen matrix. Antialiasing may even make the problem worse, for example, lines of uniform thickness might be displayed with different widths depending on their position on the screen. When designing icons, the design should always be optimised for a specific size in pixels, which will be determined by the device.

The exact size at which the icons are to be displayed should be checked very carefully. Alterations may be necessary and it is sometimes helpful to correct the size by adding or removing one pixel in order to achieve precise corners – a missing corner pixel can create the impression of a rounded corner.

Glossary

Font standards

Postscript fonts are a uniform digital font standard. A Postscript font consists of two files: one file has the bitmap for the screen and the other has the vector data which the printer can use to implement the font.

TrueType fonts are a platform dependent digital standard. Here, the outline component and the screen display are contained in a single file.

TrueType ESQ (Enhanced Screen Quality) fonts are TrueType fonts which are especially optimised for display on screens.

OpenType fonts are a cross-platform font solution as they can be displayed both on PCs and Macs. OpenType fonts are optimised for the internet and online publications, and can be embedded in files.

Typographical terms

Tracking describes the proportional distance between all characters. The tracking value can be changed and, it is advisable to increase the tracking slightly for small type with antialiasing to prevent the letters from running together.

Kerning refers to the varying distance between any two individual characters. This laborious, fine-tuning technique is only worth employing for features such as menu item labels and icons.

Leading refers to the distance between one line and the next. Here, again, the standard value is optimised for printing on paper. For screen purposes, the leading should be increased slightly if possible.

Hinting refers to the careful modification of fonts and is implemented in the font set. It ensures that the font is optimally displayed on the screen, even in small type sizes.

Data formats

ASCII (American Standard Code for Information Interchange) is the de facto standard in which the binary code for each letter is defined.

Bitmap is a file format that stores the information about an object in a matrix. Each cell of the matrix corresponds to a value that can be expressed in bits. Bitmap files cannot be increased in size without a loss of quality. GIF, JPG and TIFF are bitmap file formats.

Vector is a file format that stores graphics in the form of a geometrical description. Vector graphics can be magnified without any loss of quality. When they are reduced in size, the automatic implementation on the pixel matrix of the screen may be imprecise. Vector formats include EPS and SWF.

TXT is a text file that does not contain any formatting.

RTF (Rich Text Format) is a file that contains information about font and layout.

JPEG (Joint Photographic Experts Group) is a common file format for image data. It is available at various levels of compression.

TIFF (Tagged Image File Format) is a very common file format for high quality image material. It does not generate any artificial compression and is mainly used in the print sector.

GIF (Graphic Interchange Format) is a file format for image data. It generates small files, but it only has a maximum of 256 available colours. One colour can be used as a transparency channel.

PDF (Portable Document Format) is a file format that offers a digital counterpart to the printed version of a document.

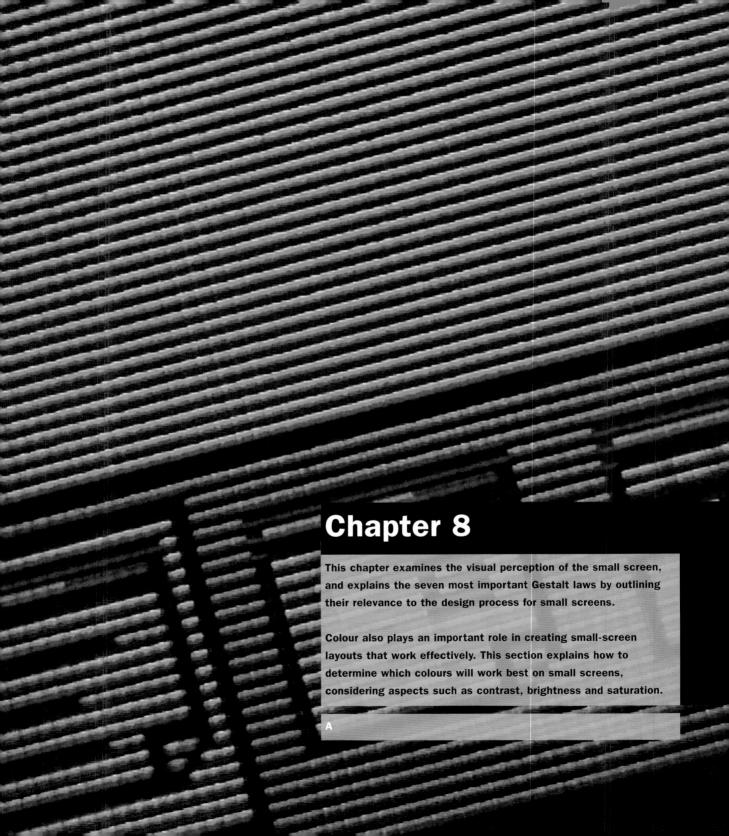

Chapter 8

This chapter examines the visual perception of the small screen, and explains the seven most important Gestalt laws by outlining their relevance to the design process for small screens.

Colour also plays an important role in creating small-screen layouts that work effectively. This section explains how to determine which colours will work best on small screens, considering aspects such as contrast, brightness and saturation.

A

Layout and Colour on Small Screens

This section shows examples of small-screen interfaces that use sophisticated colour palettes, which guide the user and support the content.

The example of a well-designed mobile phone demonstrates that a holistic approach to the design process can generate great small-screen designs.

In this section we outline the basics about the additive colour system and colour depth, and provide information about the available colour depth on small-screen displays.

B

C

The design of small-screen interfaces is subject to the same basic design principles and considerations as those that apply to larger screens. However, the available space is much smaller, and this limits the visual effect of the screen, because it only occupies a small part of the user's field of vision. Design principles and techniques must therefore be used in a clear and logical manner so that the user can quickly grasp the underlying functionality. This means that all design resources must serve to visualise information, structure the content and the interaction possibilities before any decorative and illustration aspects are considered. An exception must be made for entertainment applications, which are used for leisure purposes and as such are given far greater attention and concentration by the user.

Visual perception and the small screen

The Gestalt laws are a series of rules that formulate the psychological perception characteristics of human beings. A designer can and should use these principles to organise information logically so that the user can understand content quickly and clearly. The Gestalt laws are also helpful as a guideline for the presentation of information on small-screen interfaces. The following seven laws summarise the most important principles of perception, and how they affect the design considerations of small-screen interfaces.

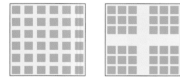

Organisation of the content by **proximity**.

The law of **proximity** states that elements which are arranged closely together are perceived as a group or unit. This principle can be used in the design of screens to organise the content and create units with a common meaning. However, this design resource can only be used to a limited extent on small screens due to the lack of available space; allowing large gaps between different units in order to separate them visually would waste valuable screen space. Usually it is sensible to combine this principle with the principle of similarity.

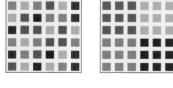

The law of **similarity** maintains that elements with similar properties are perceived as belonging to a group or unit. This principle can be used to set apart interactive elements such as icons or to create units of meaning, for example, by displaying related items in the same colour. The principle is unaffected by scale, and therefore it is the most important organisational resource for small-screen designs.

Organisation of the content by **similarity** can also be combined with the principle of proximity.

The law of **closure** states that our perception skills will supplement incomplete elements. This unconscious process can be used to create a visual link between the soft keys positioned on the hardware and the functions that are displayed on the screen.

An important factor for the designer to note is that of all geometrical figures, the circle is the element that is visually most robust. Even if only fractions of the circle are present, the shape will be automatically completed by the human perception system.

Semantic grouping by geometrical supplementation.

The law of **good form** maintains that human perception will look for the greatest degree of simplicity, clarity and regularity and then interpret this form as a coherent element.

This principle can be applied deliberately, but it can also occur accidentally if random common structures are incorporated within different on-screen elements, as this will confuse the user and give the impression of a connection that is not there. In the design process, care should be taken to ensure that no unintended meta-structures occur that would make reading the information more difficult.

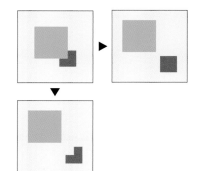

The arrangement at the top left can be perceived as being a combination of two different components, depending on the way in which it is viewed.

According to the law of good form the arrangement at the top right is the most simplified interpretation and as such will be regarded as the 'correct' version by the user.

If the configuration shown at bottom left is actually the correct interpretation, a gap should then be left between the two components to ensure it is viewed as intended by the designer.

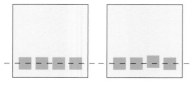

Activation of elements can be indicated visually by departing from the regular form.

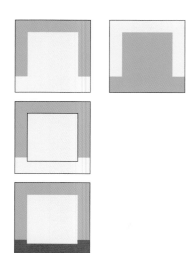

Symmetry can be used to create a relationship between the content of virtual and physical elements.

The law of **symmetry** or **regularity** asserts the tendency of human perception to search for regular forms. These regular patterns can be created by equal gaps or by mirrored axes. A design that complies with this law is generally regarded as harmonious and balanced. In screen design it is sensible to take this need for harmony into account – alternatively it can be violated deliberately in order to focus the user's attention or provide some form of warning information.

The law of **figure/ground** states that a striking element will be perceived as the relevant form, and any surrounding space is considered to be the background. If the relationship between the fore- and background is not clear, the user may be left confused and the elements displayed will be regarded as ambiguous.

This principle must be taken into account in screen design whenever there is any overlap between elements. Pop-up menus, pull-down menus and windows should all be designed so that they are clearly in the foreground of the display. This effect can be achieved by using brightness and contrast levels to set the foreground clearly apart from the background.

Where there is **overlap** between elements, the foreground should be brighter than the background to make the interpretation clear. To enhance this, it is also possible to temporarily darken the background or reduce its contrast.

Basic design exercise

Find one example of each of the seven Gestalt laws on the screen interface of a mobile phone.

Evaluate the application of each of the laws and ascertain whether the interface could be designed in a more striking or effective manner.

The law of **continuity** maintains that the human perception system does not analyse each new component afresh, but instead draws conclusions based on what it has already seen or experienced. This principle can be observed, for example, when we read a word that has been spelt incorrectly; the meaning of the word is likely to be plain from the context, and so the error will not impinge our understanding of the text. Our ability to complete visual patterns means that a user can understand abbreviated text and concepts, and this can be exploited and used to save space on small-screen designs.

The law of continuity also applies to the dimension of time. Similar images seen in quick succession, one after the other, are perceived as being in motion (this is the principle on which animation is based). It is important to remember that this inertia of human perception must always be taken into account. Therefore, warning information should always contrast clearly with the standard display information on the screen so that it is not overlooked by the user.

The law of continuity can be developed even further in interactive processes such as using a mobile phone: the user's actions should be interpreted into plausible reactions by the interface and these should continue the direction, radius and intensity of the movement by an appropriate animation on the screen.

For more on the subject of continuity, see also 'instant feedback' and 'natural mapping' in Chapter 3: Physical Interaction.

Digseinng for the Slaml Sneecrs... Arcdicnog to a sdtuy at Cmabridge Uinervtisty, it dseno't mteatr waht oedrr the lterets in a wrod are in, as lnog as the fsrit and lsat lteetr are in the rhgit pitoosin. The rset can be celtplomey meixd up, and it can slitl be esaliy raed busecae the hmaun bairn rdaes the wrod as a wlohe, not eervy snlige ltteer.

peds	–	pedestrians
xing	–	crossing
prkwy	–	parkway

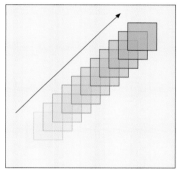

A sequence of similar images creates the **illusion of motion**.

Nowadays smaller screens can display an increasing number of colours. Originally only black and white was available; this progressed to greyscale, and then colour screens. The first colour displays only had a limited range of 16 colours, but nowadays 18 bit screens with more than 200,000 colour shades are available. It is likely that true colour, with its colour depth capacity of 24 bit or 32 bit, will soon be available for use on small-screen devices, thus providing designers the same colour capabilities that they have on larger screens.

When selecting colours for the digital medium, the **intrinsic brightness** of colours in the RGB colour scale must be taken into account – these are different from the brightness effect of CMYK colours.

This difference cannot be shown adequately in print, so the shift in contrast is demonstrated here with a brightness scale.

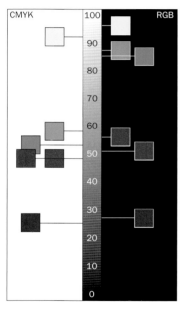

Colour on small screens

Some of the first colour screens used very strong colours; the possibility of using colour led to much exaggeration and a number of almost overpowering initial designs. The fact that small-screen devices are used for shorter periods and with less user concentration than their full-sized counterparts means that the designer must primarily use colour as a means to make the operation of the device as simple as possible. Therefore, colour should be used to direct the user's focus so that they can quickly distinguish what is important and what is unimportant and so be swifter to make their interaction decisions.

The effect of colour **contrast and brightness** also plays an important role on small-screen interfaces. To understand the interaction concept, the screen must be easy to read, even under adverse conditions. An important consideration for legibility on both large and small screens is the contrast in brightness.

Colour is displayed on the screen by mixing the three primary colours of red, green and blue in an additive mixture. Colours generated by additive colour mixing are characterised by the fact that their resulting secondary colours will be significantly brighter than the primary colours because extra light will have been transmitted. This will serve to exaggerate or distort the intrinsic brightness of colour families, and affects the contrasts between different colours and combinations of colour on the screen. An absolute brightness contrast of 50% should be exceeded for all important content on the screen.

The **absolute brightness contrast** should always be more than 50%; if necessary this value should be checked by converting the colours to a greyscale.

Brightness and contrast can be used systematically to enhance the the depth of the screen. This means that content that is in the background or is currently inactive should appear darker in colour and with lower contrast and colour saturation. Content that is currently in use, such as dialogue windows or pop-up menus, should appear brighter and have higher contrast and colour saturation. These principles support figure/ground perception and also help the user to grasp the structure and the focus of interaction quickly.

Spatial impact can be further enhanced by a systematic selection of the colour family. Cold colours can be used to visually form the background, whereas warmer colours tend to appear in the foreground and closer to the user.

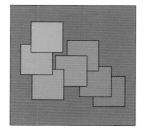
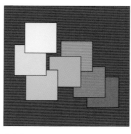
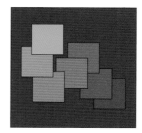

saturation   brightness + saturation   brightness

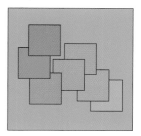

There are also physiological reasons that affect the choice of colour.

See also Section C in Chapter 8.

154|155 >

cold/warm   brightness + saturation + cold/warm

To check the contrast and brightness that a design offers, it is helpful to convert it to greyscale. This enables the designer to check the values irrespective of the colours selected. See also Section A in Chapter 9 for other prototyping techniques.

158|159 >

Basic design exercise
Develop a colour scheme that allows three different hierarchical levels to be displayed simultaneously. Then find a suitable colour with which text can be displayed so that it is clearly legible.

8A   8B   8C

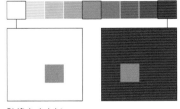

Shift in brightness.

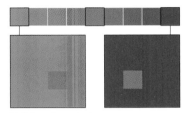

Shift in colour shade.

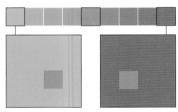

Saturation shift.

Another colour principle that must be taken into account when designing screen interfaces is **simultaneous contrast**. This describes a shift in the perceived colour value, and plays an important role in the legibility of a colour code. Depending on the colour environment, a shade can shift in such a way that it may no longer be clearly assigned. Dark blue on a white background, for example, may be difficult to differentiate from black on a white background. Equally, what at first appears to be a neutral grey colour may unintentionally appear as a violet colour if it is displayed next to green.

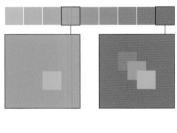

The **saturation of a colour** on the luminescent medium of a screen must be used very sparingly. The rule of thumb is that the larger the surface area, and the longer the time spent looking at the screen, then the less saturated the colour should be. If this is not adhered to, the user's eyes may become tired and this can lead to unpleasant afterimages. If colour saturation is used sparingly, an increase in saturation can then be used to mark different priorities in the content.

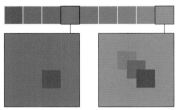

An increase in saturation can be used to attract the user's eye.

It is very useful to use **colour for coding** purposes. Colour can represent a code for different action routines, for example, green for approval, red for rejection and yellow for warnings. Colour can also be used to distinguish different types of content or applications. However, human beings do not have an absolute colour memory, so only a limited number of clearly distinguishable colours should be used in any one design; the colours should then be supplemented by an alternative form of identification such as an icon. Problems can arise if colour coding is used simultaneously for routine actions and content categories within an application.

The colour selection and scales used must be clearly distinguishable in order to avoid confusion, for example, by using less saturated colour shades on larger background areas to mark the categories, and using fewer highly-saturated colours to denote routine actions.

A unique problem on small-screen devices is that the available space in which to display colours greatly limits the perception of the colour shade. The smaller the area that is to be highlighted, the clearer the colours must be in the colour code, which means that the number of available colours is lower.

	full	go	yes
	medium		maybe
	empty	stop	no

Colour codes such as the **traffic light** analogy are clearly visible and easy to understand even on small screens.

To ensure that colours can be easily distinguished, they must be displayed on a surface that is large enough: the more subtle the colour, the larger the space needed to display it.

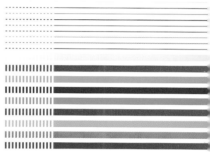

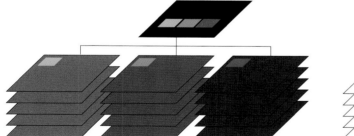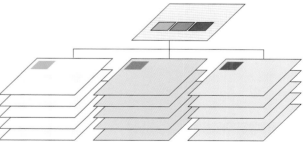

All known colour contrasts become greater on the luminescent medium of a screen. Every colour and design concept should therefore be tested at real size and in different lighting conditions. See also Chapter 9: Developing Designs for Small Screens.

The evolution of colour displays has vastly increased the range of possibilities open to the designer. In many cases, the opportunity to use colour has led to brightly coloured screens that seem to follow the logic that excess is preferable.

Colour is often used to decorate the screen interface, but at the lower levels of navigation the design is still dominated by long monochrome lists. With the greater colour capability, however, it is possible to incorporate more subtle shades and gradations, and these are increasingly used for functional purposes.

Skin designs for the main menu level of a mobile phone (Panasonic competition, 2004): the selected icon is highlighted by an animation, which creates a further contrast by size. The activation is also highlighted by a contrast between colour and grey.

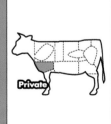

The selected icons are highlighted by placing them on different coloured areas.

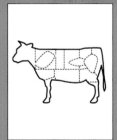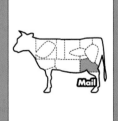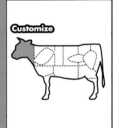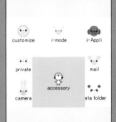

The more conventional the navigation is, the greater the scope to use formal variations without confusing the user.

NTT DoCoMo Flash Website: this is the portal for the Japanese mobile phone network operator NTT DoCoMo. As the lightest colour in the chromatic circle, yellow is very suitable and popular as a highlighting colour on screen displays. Here the activation is coded both by colour and by a change of size.

au Website: this portal for the Japanese mobile phone network operator au by KDDI, uses a colour scheme which is similar to that of its competitor: NTT DoCoMo.

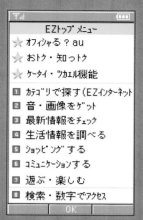

149 mm x 71 mm

Navigation System AVIC N1 (Pioneer): here, the staggered display of the approaching exit roads is underlined by a reduction in the colour saturation. This corresponds to natural perspective vision.

SO506iC (Sony Ericsson): varying the contrast is an effective way to guide the user's eyes and enable them to distinguish what is important and unimportant, and active or inactive.

Navigation System 750NAVplus (Magellan): a contrast between the grey and coloured elements helps the user to distinguish the contextual information from their route at a glance.

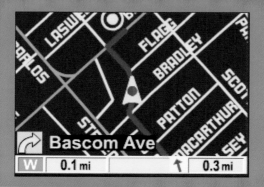

8A

8B

8C

Initially relatively little effort was made in the design of small-screen interfaces. However, it is now generally accepted that the attractiveness and user-friendliness of the interface represent a major factor to the commercial success of the device. This has lead to a new professionalism and vigour in the design of the software.

The Dream Project developed a set of 16 demo websites, which incorporated mobile, web and video applications, to showcase the capabilities of Adobe GoLive CS2. The website designs reflect plausible business models and familiar m-commerce scenarios in order to encourage Adobe's customers to adapt the designs to their own specific requirements. The mobile phone models include the Sony Ericsson and Nokia feature phones, and the Symbian OS smart phones.

The Dream Project 'Oeno' (2004): this is a design concept for a mobile wine guide. A clear colour code helps the user to distinguish between the sections for white and red wines. (The dream project: Adobe Systems, twenty2product and George Williams)

W21K (Kyocera): here the full spectrum is used to colour code all twelve menu items. Since the colours are so close on the colour wheel they are only distinguishable in direct visual comparison. Therefore icons and text are used as redundant coding.

K700i (Sony Ericsson): blue is the predominant colour choice for display backgrounds. This is because all shades of blue will stay visually in the background, and as such provide the perfect canvas for warmer tones that will automatically move towards the viewer's attention.

T-Mobile Flash: a news page on various topics, all of which are distinguished by colour codes.

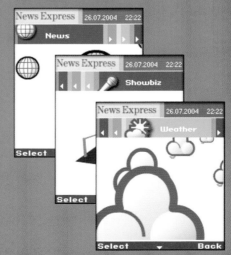

97 mm x 71 mm

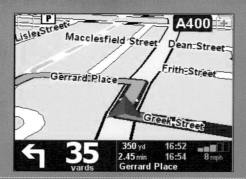

XY-Watch: this is a timepiece concept that offers an alternative presentation of time. The 24 hours of a day are shown on the vertical axis, and the minutes of each hour are shown on the horizontal axis. The resulting coloured rectangles on the screen therefore constantly change their proportions and are reminiscent of the ever-changing shadows cast by buildings.
(Erik Adigard, M-A-D, 2002)

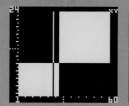

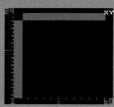

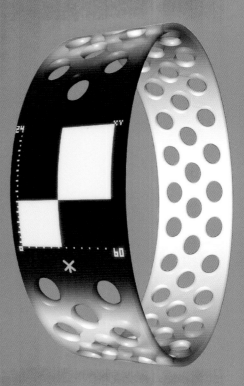

The design of small mobile devices has now reached a certain degree of maturity. This allows projects to be realised in which the physical product form and the interface are designed together and with equal care. The result of these projects is almost always a distinctly simple product with an equally minimalist design.

Talby Mobile Phone (2004): this was created by the product designer Marc Newson for the Japanese network operator au by KDDI.

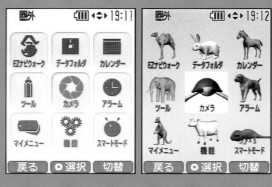

The system architecture follows a classical breakdown into nine menus, and a flat, monochrome design of the icons with a high level of graphical abstraction that is reminiscent of wood carvings. Some icons are innovative in their motif, such as the image of a camera shutter to denote the 'photograph' menu.

It is possible to choose different display options that are way beyond common 'skin' concepts. For example, the main menu can be displayed in the 3x3 menu matrix or as a list. Both arrangements have various differently designed alternative interfaces.

Alternative menu screens, screensavers and time presentations all have a high design quality and make optimum use of the resolution and colour quality of the hardware.

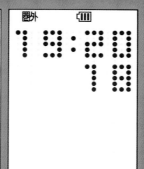

In all of the menus, the depth of the colour in the display is used to implement subtle colour gradations. This almost monochrome appearance gives the device a high quality appearance, which represents a pleasant change from the brightly coloured standard encountered on most devices.

The individual categories are supported by a colour code, but the range of colours in the code is only slightly saturated. However, if the respective colour is used over a relatively large area, the colour shades can be easily distinguished. As a result, it is still possible to use highly saturated colours in small quantities to show functions that apply across the category boundaries.

Small screens are backlit or 'luminescent' media that work on the principle of **additive colour mixing**. The most widespread types are LCD displays. These have a slightly reduced colour range and contrast than tube monitors. This is due to the even backlighting, which brightens the dark parts of the image.

In the presentation of motion, the adaptation speed of LCDs has almost reached that of tube monitors. The slight motion blur that results from the inertia of LCD crystals is negligible in the reproduction of moving pictures on small-screen displays.

Additive colour mixing: on LCD displays, all of the colours are created by combinations of three adjacent sub-pixels in the primary colours of red, green and blue.

The **colour depth** available on small screens is constantly increasing. The processor power and battery capacity will determine exactly what depth is possible, but most colour displays will soon offer at least 18 bit colour depth, which results in 262,144 available colours.

In practical design work, greater colour depth means that more individual colour shades are available. For example, colour gradations can only be displayed satisfactorily with a colour depth of 16 bits or higher. This is an important factor both in the design of three-dimensional elements and in the reproduction of images and moving pictures.

A colour depth of **one bit** means that only two states are available: 'on' or 'off'.

A 12 bit colour depth means that each of the red, green and blue sub-pixels can take on 16 different brightness levels. This results in 4,096 colour shades, which each individual pixel can assume.

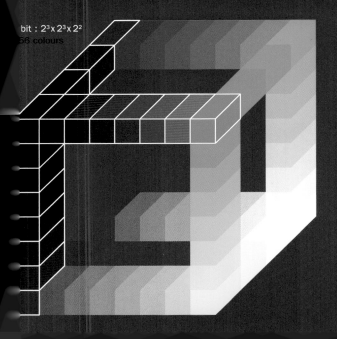

bit : $2^3 \times 2^3 \times 2^2$
56 colours

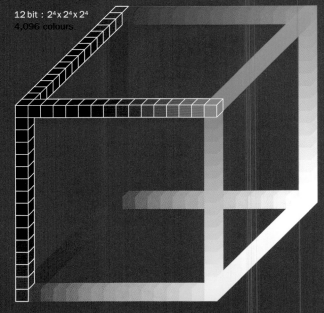

12 bit : $2^4 \times 2^4 \times 2^4$
4,096 colours

Human beings can see light across a **spectrum** of 380 to 780 nanometres. Brightness is registered by the **rods**, whereas colour is perceived by three different types of **cones**. The red cones are most sensitive to long light wavelengths (565 nm), the green cones to average light wavelengths (535 nm) and the blue cones (440 nm) to short light wavelengths. The cones are not evenly distributed on the retina; there are significantly fewer blue cones than green and red cones; and blue cones are only situated at the periphery of the field of vision.

For sharp display of light with different colours, and thus different wavelengths, various adjustments must be made in the lens curvature. The characteristics of the human vision system mean that small blue objects, such as blue text, are difficult to view sharply and tend to appear blurred – this explains why blue is so popular as a background colour. Blue is felt to be the colour that is least forceful and disturbing because the human eye does not perceive this colour so intensively.

Cones

Rods

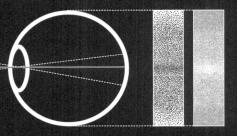

For some colour depths, the number of bits is not evenly distributed between the three primary colours. This is due to the unit convention of binary calculation. However, this slight distortion in the colours is beyond the perception abilities of the lay person.

16 bit : $2^5 \times 2^6 \times 2^5$
65,536 colours

18 bit : $2^6 \times 2^6 \times 2^6$
262,144 colours

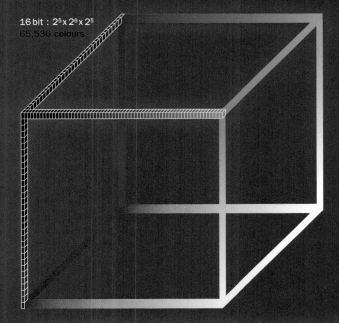

Chapter 9

This chapter introduces methods and techniques such as paper prototyping and software prototyping with authoring tools, which will allow you to plan, visualise and test small-screen designs.

A

Developing Designs for Small Screens

The second section of this chapter presents two examples that demonstrate the broad range of challenges which arise when designing a small-screen interface. The first example is a location-based service on a hand-held device, and the second example is a multimedia interface designed for an automotive application.

In this section we summarise various tips, hints, resources and software that help the designer to plan and prototype small-screen interface designs.

B

C

The planning and design of branched-feedback processes is very complex. As such the accompanying design process must be iterative: every hypothesis must first be discussed between all the disciplines involved and then continually revised. There are working techniques that can be employed to facilitate the exchange of ideas so that practitioners from varied disciplines, for example, psychologists, economists, information architects, interface designers, graphic designers, computer programmers and engineers, can all work effectively together.

The scenario

In order to develop an application that takes the needs of potential users into account in its range of functions and its navigation structure, it is helpful to prepare potential usage scenarios. With the aid of a speculative and detailed description of a probable usage concept, a list of the requirements for an application can be formulated in a fairly precise manner. This technique helps to define priorities in a navigation structure, and develop realistic situational interaction concepts, because they are projected on to an individual with a wide range of characteristics, rather than a stereotype focus group.

The paper computer

Simulating an application on paper is a way to quickly gain insights and implement various actions from the digital world in a simple and efficient manner. A paper computer contains all of the planned interactive elements that are to be incorporated in the application, but here they are made of paper and to scale. Typical usage scenarios and user types of the application are then simulated with this 'software'. Alternative layouts can be experimented with for the screen and missing interactive elements or gaps in user interaction logic can easily be identified.

The fact that this takes place outside the digital arena encourages practitioners from a variety of disciplines to ignore the potential technical limitations and instead focus on a solution that best suits the content. The technique of the paper computer can be used at the start of the project development, but it can also be employed at any time during the development process for critical review or correction.

When an interface is developed on a screen, one complicating factor is that the resolution of the screen is rarely the same as the resolution of the end device. This means that interactive elements are almost always smaller in the final version than they appear to be on the screen in the design and editing phase. For this reason the full-scale simulation of elements in a paper computer is of decisive importance in the development process of small-screen devices.

The organisational diagram

The visualisation of navigation levels and links within an application will play a crucial role in the development, design and communication of the interaction concept and the information architecture. Even though it is not always easy to visualise branched-feedback processes on a two-dimensional surface, an organisational diagram of the application as a whole is a central planning tool that unites all the disciplines involved. The specification details of a screen surface can only be designed when all the functions of an application have been integrated and recorded in this structural plan.

There are no established or binding coding standards for the presentation of organisational diagrams, and they are one of the interaction methods that designers can use to convincingly present their concept of the 'look and feel' of an application. This method is particularly suitable if a great deal of work needs to be invested in the technical implementation in order to achieve a particularly convenient and visually convincing interface.

Simulation

Various techniques can be used to simulate an application. In addition to the animation of a sample sequence, interactive demonstrations can be created with varying degrees of realism. These simulations can be programmed with a number of authoring programs, such as Macromedia Director. The type of simulation created will depend on the questions that need to be answered by the demonstration. For example, if the mode of interaction is to be tested, then the physical input element and the system's corresponding reaction should work as realistically as possible. In this simulation, the design of the screen will play a subordinate role. Equally, if the intuitive use of a navigation structure is to be tested, a computer simulation of this can be a suitable demonstration method. If the legibility is to be tested, the presentation must be checked on an original display.

Evaluation

Demonstrations and prototypes not only provide insight for the designer, but they can also be used to enable others to critically evaluate the work in progress. Depending on the scope of the project, this can be achieved via extensive surveys of the target group or in small-scale tests with members of the development team. Problems of interaction and understanding can be identified, and eventually resolved, and this helps to optimise the design concept.

In the development of software applications for small-screen devices, the interaction steps must be planned with the caveat that the user is liable to be impatient and/or distracted when using the product. This means that functions must be analysed carefully to determine how often they are used and how easily a user can reach them within the navigation structure. The more often a function is needed, the more accessible it must be. Usage scenarios will help to indicate cross-references in the navigation structure, and to design meaningful context menus.

This is an example of a **paper computer** city guide, which has location-based service functions for a hand-held computer. All of the interface elements, such as tabulators for the search categories and the available tools, are made of paper. The different layers of information that can be displayed on a city map are simulated with transparent paper.
(Interactive guide, Susanne Stage, 2003)

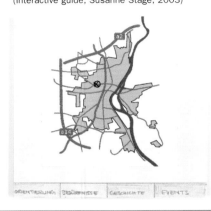

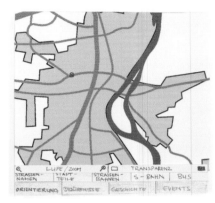

Activis Scheduler: using the daily schedule of a notional person, alternative designs were developed for the layout and presentation of time and location information on this device. The simulated designs are produced as bitmap graphics to give a realistic impression of the presentation at the available resolution.
(Hendrik Rieß, 2005)

58 mm x 77 mm

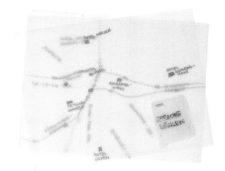

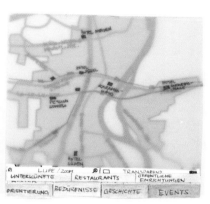

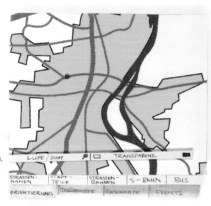

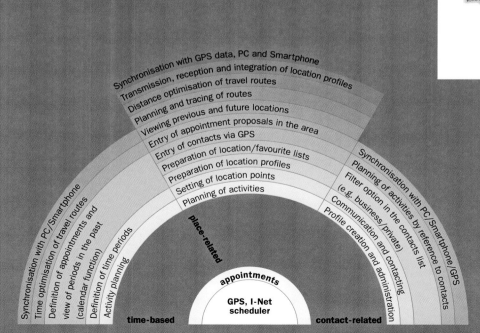

Synchronisation with GPS data, PC and Smartphone

Transmission, reception and integration of location profiles

Distance optimisation of travel routes

Planning and tracing of routes

Viewing previous and future locations

Entry of appointment proposals in the area

Entry of contacts via GPS

Preparation of location/favourite lists

Preparation of location profiles

Setting of location points

Planning of activities

Synchronisation with PC/Smartphone

Time optimisation of travel routes

Definition of appointments and view of periods in the past (calendar function)

Definition of time periods

Activity planning

Synchronisation of activities with PC/Smartphone/GPS

Planning of activities by reference to contacts

Filter option in the contacts list (e.g. business/private)

Communication and contacting

Profile creation and administration

place-related

appointments

GPS, I-Net scheduler

time-based

contact-related

Activis Scheduler: this is the organisational diagram of the software. This diagram arranges the functions of the application by user priority.
(Hendrik Rieß, 2005)

**Christian Langer, Lapavalley GmbH,
The Creation of a Multimedia Guide to Marwell Zoo,
Winchester, UK**

"

*Multimedia guides for museums, exhibitions and similar venues were already a subject of discussion in 2002. So when we founded our company, we realised that we needed to set ourselves apart from potential competitors and find our own market niche. We developed the idea of producing mobile multimedia guides for zoos, animal parks and aquariums.
To be as convincing in our acquisition of clients, we designed a realistic demonstration guide.*

To make a name for ourselves, we sent a brochure describing the exact functions of our guide to almost all the zoos in the UK. We were fortunate to receive a positive response fairly quickly: Marwell Zoological Park in Winchester was interested.

In an initial meeting we presented our demonstration guide to the zoo's Director, Deputy Director, Marketing and Promotion Officer and Head of Education. The reactions were very positive, but we were not able to remove all doubts about this new technology. Marwell was very interested, but the zoo was not keen to be the first zoo in the UK to bear the full risk of funding such a project. However, we wanted to preserve our chance to implement the pilot project as far as possible.

After brief negotiations, the two parties came to the following agreement: Marwell was willing to fund the hardware, and we were willing to develop the software, free of charge, as our share of the risk. The potential revenue from hiring the device to visitors was then to be shared.

Marwell was very cooperative in the organisation of the content and the interface design. Of course the guide needed to fit in with the existing corporate design, but otherwise we largely had a free hand and were able to experiment with the system in the location until we, along with the voluntary testers and the responsible parties, were finally satisfied.

The picture material that Marwell sent to us in the form of a VHS video and some photo CDs proved to be almost redundant. There was obviously some confusion about the entertaining and instructive potential of our multimedia guides – after all, a visitor does not want to see a video clip of a sleeping panther if he is standing in front of the enclosure in which the same panther is sleeping.

So we decided to produce the picture content ourselves. We went inside a number of animal enclosures, hid the feed of big cats inside jute sacks, stroked rhinos, tapirs, bird-eating spiders and more, and we recorded everything on video or by taking photographs. We also interviewed some keepers, and we accompanied the vet on his rounds. After a week we had collected enough material to fill the guide with exciting and informative content.

Initially we had problems with the hardware. The PDAs had to be enclosed in a waterproof covering so that they could survive both wet weather and accidental submersion in the penguin pool! However, the plastic waterproof bags with transparent windows, which were specially made for the device, had a detrimental effect on the contrast of the displays, and this effect was exacerbated in bright sunlight. After two weeks of conducting usability tests carried out with volunteers from all age groups, it was clear that the contrast of all graphics had to be enhanced in order to ensure their legibility.

In August 2003 we launched our first multimedia guide, almost ten months after our first contact with Marwell. Now the devices have been in operation for more than two years, and all parties are more than satisfied with the results. The number of units hired out per quarter shows very clearly that our work was worthwhile and visitors to Marwell have enthusiastically received the guide.

"

56.4 mm x 56.4 mm

Shown left are the **preliminary designs** for the interface of the guide. The interactive buttons are highlighted by their plasticity.

Shown right are the **final designs** of the interface. A brightness gradation creates depth and helps to emphasise the option buttons.

A variety of applications are being developed for a number of new mobile services. Often, persuading the client of their significance will be just as important in these projects as their technical feasibility.

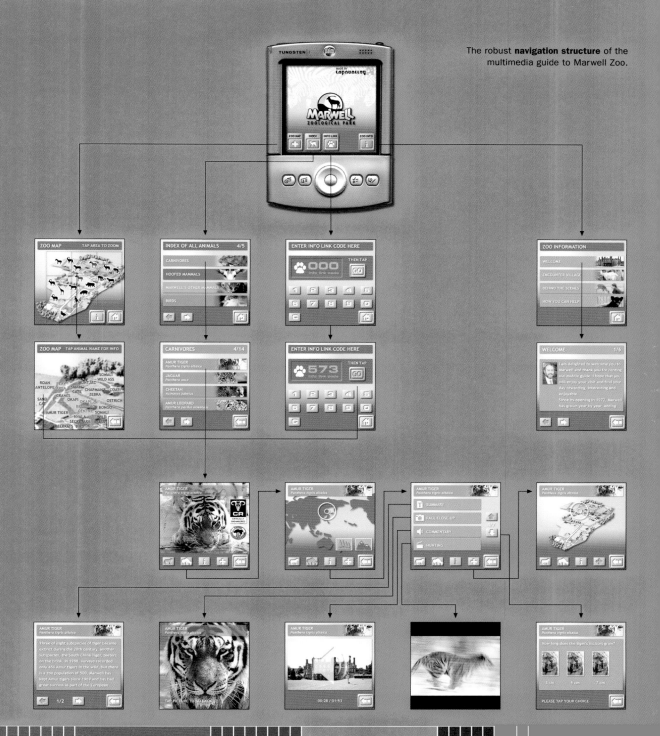

The robust **navigation structure** of the multimedia guide to Marwell Zoo.

Small screens are not only incorporated in individual mobile devices, but they also form the user interface for an increasing number of products that are used in everyday life. Integration of a small-screen device in the car is a unique challenge because a driver will not primarily concentrate on using the display – the focus will instead be fixed on the road ahead.

To link the rotation of the control unit as closely as possible with the display on the screen, vertical lists and selection options are arranged on segments of a circle, or around its circumference.

**Gerhard Mauter, Head of Development MMI at Audi AG,
The Development of a Multimedia Interface for the A8**

How were the concepts simulated or communicated in the initial phase of the project?

"Simulation was initially carried out with a PC, and in the second stage a sitting duck was used that already integrated the real display and a prototype of the control unit. Then a predecessor model to the A8 was equipped with a display and control unit in the constellation that was planned for mass production. The control unit and display were operated by means of a PC, which was installed in the boot of the car and this enabled specific functions to be simulated. The radio only had a fixed list of stations, the sound was generated with .wav files and the CDs, TV and navigation system were simulated. The telephone worked properly, including the telephone lists and voice control.

During the development we used every opportunity to demonstrate the progress of the work to all of the directors and to important decision-makers so that they would have the opportunity to contribute their ideas at an early stage."

The interaction is optionally either via
an operating panel in the central console
or with keys and scroll wheels that are
integrated into the steering wheel.

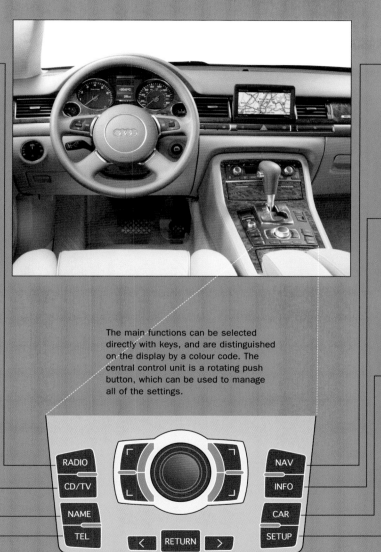

The main functions can be selected
directly with keys, and are distinguished
on the display by a colour code. The
central control unit is a rotating push
button, which can be used to manage
all of the settings.

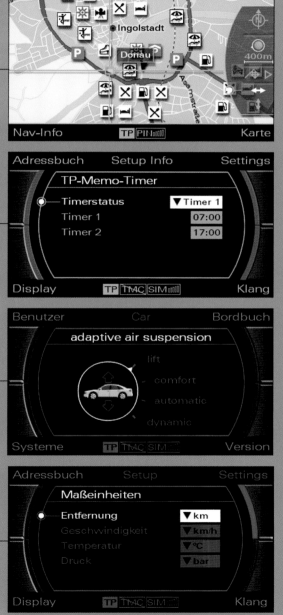

By contrast with applications that are developed for a personal computer, the designer of any interactive system which is to be implemented in an object of everyday use cannot assume their potential users will be familiar with how computers or computer applications work.

Global products need localised interfaces. The concept must take into account the space required by different languages, and this must be tested in sample layouts.

What were the greatest challenges?

Reaching a consensus in the development team. The interdisciplinary make-up of the MMI team included specialists from areas such as design, technology and ergonomics.

Creating a mental model in a short time that would enable the later users to quickly learn how to operate the system.

Finding a middle solution in the reduction of keys to keep the learning threshold as low as possible for the customer – because customers are always intimidated by such a new system.

For many development engineers it was removing a whole range of functions from direct access and integrating them into the menu control.

The internal interlinking between the operating concept, the design, the hardware and software development – and organising the external interaction of development suppliers. For example, this included the definition of the interfaces; here we used completely new methods of software specification by including illustrated organisational diagrams: StateCharts.

For me personally, the development of the central rotating control unit was one of the greatest challenges. It took three years before this control unit achieved its physical quality and its tactile attractiveness.

In what ways was the concept evaluated?

When our decision-makers were involved in the course of the internal communication process, we also used them to check the usability of the system because they perfectly match the profile of our A8 customers. There were also several expert reports from recognised authorities in the area of control concepts, and we conducted smaller internal usability tests. A large-scale usability test with almost 100 external potential customers (the oldest of whom was 72 years old), also provided a number of suggestions, and most of them were implemented in the final product.

Driving trials were held at a very early stage of the development to help select the input elements. Criteria such as the speed of entries and error frequency were logged. Different input elements such as arrow keys, a touchscreen and a revolving knob were compared.

As such typical computer interactions and functional concepts cannot be taken for granted in the development of interaction concepts. The designer must ensure that these concepts provide independent and robust mental models, which are easy to learn and these must be carefully tested with potential user groups.

A common problem occurs with displays that do not consist of square pixels. Here, the design must first be compressed by the appropriate factor so that it is shown in the right proportions on the target display. In the instance of circular forms and text display, it is very noticeable if the proportions are not right.

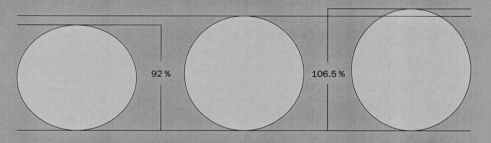

92 %   106.5 %

155 mm x 88 mm

Benutzer   Car   Bordbuch

Warnschwelle

80
km/h

30   240

Systeme   TP TMC SIM   Version

In the creation of small-screen applications, the designer must show great flexibility and be constantly open to new concepts and techniques. This is partly because elements such as screen size, resolution and colour depth are constantly changing and partly because the forms of interaction and operating systems for small-screen devices are not as standardised as they are for personal computers.

For these reasons, careful research into the technical specifications is always essential in the concept development and the design of applications.

Authoring Programs: such as Macromedia Director enable interactive systems to be simulated and they can also be used to produce software prototypes for small screens. These programs are easy for designers to use, and they offer three important functions. Firstly, the simulation provides the designer with insight; secondly, they allow the designer to create impressive presentations, and finally, authoring programs can create prototypes that can be used to test the application on potential users.

Development Environments: exist for systems such as the Palm OS; they simulate both the end device and the interface elements that are provided by the operating system. Development environments are usually complicated to handle, and therefore are more suitable for programmers.

Development Software: such as Flash Lite allows the creation of applications for small devices. This software can be used directly to create content for small screens. The form of interaction and the design options are predefined and based on standard device types.

With all digital-simulation tools, it is important to remember that the screen resolution of the computer is usually lower than the resolution of the end device. This means that screen elements and text on the end device will appear significantly smaller than on the computer in the design phase.

Digital Tools:

MyMind is a Mac application that lets you outline ideas as diagrams
www.versiontracker.com/dyn/moreinfo/macosx/19147

Freemind is a mapping software for PC and Mac platforms
http://freemind.sourceforge.net/wiki/index.php/Main_Page

Screentools provides useful tools for 'pixelmaniacs'
www.artissoftware.com/screentools/

The Opera browser for PC and Mac platforms also offers a special preview of the
Opera browser for mobile devices.
www.opera.com

Developer Sites:

WAP (Wireless Application Protocol)
http://www-106.ibm.com/developerworks/wireless/library/wi-wapapp/?article=wi

Macromedia
www.macromedia.com/devnet/

Java
www.java.sun.com/

Sony Ericsson
http://developer.sonyericsson.com/site/global/home/p_home.jsp

Palm
www.palmsource.com/developers/

Symbian
www.symbian.com/developer/index.html

Microsoft
http://msdn.microsoft.com/developercenters/

An environment to simulate mobile devices for programming XHTML/CSS
and MMS-SMIL.
http://developer.openwave.com

Encyclopedias:

http://whatis.techtarget.com
www.webopedia.com
http://en.wikipedia.org

Applications for Small Screens:

www.handango.com
www.psiloc.com
www.avantgo.com

Platform for Small Sites:

http://209.221.153.18/smallsites/

The **tools and techniques** used to create paper prototypes are very simple: scissors, paper and a pencil! The effectiveness of this technique should not be underestimated. Usage processes can be created simply and easily, then tested and modified or rejected. Experience shows that this technique is especially suitable for multi-disciplinary teams.

Chapter 1 — Small is Beautiful

Rick Smolan I **One Digital Day** I Against All Odds Productions, Inc., 1998

Information and Communications in Japan: http://www.johotsusintokei.soumu.go.jp/whitepaper/eng/WP2004/2004-index.html
Intel – Moore's Law: http://www.intel.com/research/silicon/mooreslaw.htm
Palm Evolutionary Tree: http://palmevolution.com/

Chapter 2 — The Screen

James Foley et al I **Computer Graphics** I Addison-Wesley Publishing Company, 1996
Ben Shneiderman I **User Interface Design** I mitp-Verlag, 2002
David Skopec I **Digital Layout for the Internet and other Media** I AVA Publishing SA, 2003
Brenda Laurel I **The Art of Human-Computer Interface Design** I Addison-Wesley, 1999

Patrick Baudisch's Publications: http://www.patrickbaudisch.com/publications/index.html

Chapter 3 — Physical Interaction

Jun Rekimoto I **Tilting Operations for Small Screen Interfaces** (Tech Note) I Sony Computer Science Laboratory Inc., 1996
Eric Bergman I **Information Appliances and Beyond** I Academic Press, 2000
Scott Weiss I **Handheld Usability** I John Wiley & Sons Ltd., 2002
M. Schneider-Hufschmidt (Editor), et al I **Adaptive User Interfaces – Principles and Practice** I North-Holland, 1993

Spectronic Sidetouch Multimedia Telephone: http://www.spectronic.se/english/default.asp
Fastap: http://www.digitwireless.com/
Alpine PulseTouch: http://www.alpine-usa.com/products/leading_technology/leading_tech_iva-d300.htm
Dasher Project: http://www.inference.phy.cam.ac.uk/dasher/
Nintendo DS: http://www.nintendods.com/index.jsp
FrogPad: http://www.frogpad.com/
Anoto Pen: http://www.anoto.com/

Chapter 4 — Large Structures on Small Screens

studio 7.5 I **Navigation for the Internet and other Digital Media** I AVA Publishing, 2002
Richard Saul Wurman I **Information Anxiety 2** I Que, 2001
Edward R. Tufte I **Envisioning Information** I Graphics Press, 1990
Edward R. Tufte I **Visual Explanations** I Graphics Press, 1997
Richard Saul Wurman I **Understanding USA** I TED Conferences 1999

Chapter 5   The Network on Small Screens

Howard Rheingold | **Smart Mobs – The Next Social Revolution** | Basic Books, 2002

Visual Radio: http://www.visualradio.com/
MSN Direct: http://msndirect.com
Small Sites: http://209.221.153.18/smallsites/
DVB-H: http://www.cellular.co.za/technologies/dvb-h/dvb-h.htm
Macromedia FlashLite: http://www.macromedia.com/mobile/?promoid=AXJT

Chapter 6   Entertainment on Small Screens

Katie Salen & Eric Zimmermann | **Rules of Play – Game Design Fundamentals** | The MIT Press, 2004

Game Boy Advance – Wario Ware Twisted!: http://gba.gamespy.com/gameboy-advance/mawaru-wario-ware/
Game & Watch: http://www.1up.com/do/feature?cId=3133877
Portable Games: http://www.zonadepruebas.com/web/hardware/juegosportatiles/

Chapter 7   Digital Hieroglyphs: Text and Icons on Small Screens

Pepin van Roojen | **Mini Icons** | The Pepin Press, 2003
Steve Caplin & Alastair Campbell | **Icon Design** | Stiebner Verlag GmbH, 2001
Christine Strothotte & Thomas Strothotte | **Seeing Between the Pixels – Pictures in Interactive Systems** | Springer-Verlag, 1997

Icon Compilation: http://www.intersmash.com/300images/
History of Icons: http://www.aci.com.pl/mwichary/guidebook/articles/exclusive/onethousandsquarepixelsofcanvas
Subpixel Demonstration: http://en.wikipedia.org/wiki/Image:Subpixel_demonstration_%28Quartz%29.png

Chapter 8   Layout and Colour on Small Screens

studio 7.5 | **Digital Colour for the Internet and other Media** | AVA Publishing, 2003
Pina Lewandowsky & Francis Zeischegg | **Visuelles Gestalten mit dem Computer** | Rororo, 2002
E. Bruce Goldstein | **Wahrnehmungspsychologie** | Spektrum Akademischer Verlag, 2002

Chapter 9   Developing Designs for Small Screens

Carolyn Snyder | **Paper Prototyping** | Morgan Kaufmann Publishers, 2003
Paul Wallace et al. | **I-Mode Developer's Guide** | Addison-Wesley, 2002
Christian Lindholm et al | **Mobile Usability – How Nokia Changed the Mobile Phone** | McGraw-Hill Education, 2003
Heidi Pollock | **The End-All Guide to Small-Screen Web-Dev** | http://webmonkey.wired.com/webmonkey/04/12/index4a.html

Small is Beautiful	1A|B	**16–23**
	1C	**24–27**
The Screen	2A	**30–37**
	2B	**38–41**
	2C	**42–47**
Physical Interaction	3A	**50–63**
	3B	**64–71**
	3C	**72–73**
Large Structures on Small Screens	4A	**76–87**
	4B	**88–91**
	4C	**92–93**
The Network on Small Screens	5A	**96–99**
	5B	**100–103**
	5C	**104–105**
Entertainment on Small Screens	6A	**108–109**
	6B	**110–113**
	6C	**114–115**
Digital Hieroglyphs: Text and Icons on Small Screens	7A	**118–127**
	7B	**128–133**
	7C	**134–137**
Layout and Colour on Small Screens	8A	**138–147**
	8B	**148–153**
	8C	**154–155**
Developing Designs for Small Screens	9A	**158–159**
	9B	**160–167**
	9C	**168–169**

0-9

1G **18, 105**
2G **19, 105**
2.5G **21, 105**
3G **22, 105**
3.5G **23, 105**
3D colour LCD **22**
4G **23, 105**

A

abstraction **90–91, 124, 130–131**
acoustic feedback **60**
activation **128, 130, 142**
active matrix display **43**
additive colour mixing **144, 154**
alphabetical order **80–81, 84**
alternating display **122**
alternative designs **160, 162**
analogue **79**
animation **109, 143, 159, 162**
anoto pen **55**
antialiasing **120, 134–136**
Apple Computer **18**
Apple Macintosh **18**
application **38, 92–93, 99, 153, 158–159**
arrow buttons **34**
ASCII **137**
ASCII art **110**
augmented reality **103**
authoring program **159, 168**

B

babyface **30**
back button **61, 78, 87**
background **119, 129, 142, 145, 146, 150, 155**
bandwidth **104**
barcode **68**
battery **26–27**
bit **92–93**
bitmap **136–137**
bitmap graphics **160**
blue **144, 150, 155**
bluetooth **21, 104**
booking **98**
brightness **118, 121, 145, 146**
brightness contrast **118, 142**
brightness sensor **118**
brightness, intrinsic **121, 144**
broadband **104**
browser **104**
byte **92–93**

C

calendar **99**
camera display **38, 119**
camera phone **21, 25**
car navigation system **58, 84, 90–91**
category **80–81, 97, 98**
Cell **23**
circuits **92–93**
ClearType technology **136**

[continued]

click wheel **53, 62, 68**
CMYK **144**
collapse-to-zoom concept **40**
colour, cold/warm **145**
colour **110, 121, 129, 144–155**
colour coding **126, 131, 147, 149, 150, 153, 164–165**
colour depth **144, 148, 152–154**
colour display **20**
colour shift **146**
Commodore PET 2001 **18**
common sense **125**
communication **132–133**
communication satellite **17**
communicator **20, 25**
community **96**
computer mouse **17**
computer virus **22**
cones **155**
content **96, 99, 132–133, 145, 162**
context **78, 90–91**
context menu **33, 160**
continuous text **35**
contrast **109, 121, 129, 143–145**
control **70**
control elements **100**
convenience **97, 159**
cursor **22, 53, 77**

D

database **96–97, 98**
day mode **118**
delete **55**
demonstrator **159**
design principles **60–63**
design process **158**
design rules **99**
desktop **77**
developer sites **169**
developing **158–167**
development environment **168**
development process **162**
development software **168**
dial tone **22, 108**
dialogue **98**
dialogue boxes **30**
digital **79**
digital guide **103**
digital network **19**
digital television **23**
digital tools **168–169**
direct input **126**
direct manipulation **60**
direction key **62**
discretion **57, 118**
display properties **47**
display size **42, 58**
display technologies **46–47**
disproportional zoom **36**
distortion **78**
DMFC **27**
downloadable games **115**
DPI **42–43, 45**
drag-and-drop **55**
Dynabook **17**

dynamic **109**
dynamic icon size change **131**
dynamic organisation **40, 85**
dynamic text display **122**

E

e-ink **128**
e-mail **17**
e-paper **22, 128**
enclosing metaphor **77, 89**
energy consumption **26–27**
entertainment **68, 100, 110, 112, 140**
entertainment value **108**
ergonomic **68**
evaluation **159, 162, 166**

F

feedback **53, 54, 63, 158**
feedback, acoustic **60**
feedback, instant **60**
feedback, tactile **53, 69, 72**
fishnet concept **41**
flash (lite) **39, 149, 150, 168**
flash memory card **21**
flip zoom **36**
focus group **77, 125, 158, 167**
focus group testing **159, 166**
folder **77, 79**
folding keyboards **58**
FOMA **21**
font **110, 119–121, 128, 134–135**
font selection **134–135**
font standard **137**
foreground **142**
form **99**
fuel cell **23, 27**
fun **68, 108–115**
functions **161**

G

game **41, 71, 108, 112–114**
game & watch **18, 112**
game boy **19, 20, 112–113**
game categories **114–115**
game console **18–20, 22–23, 50, 92–93, 108**
game logic **108**
game parameters **114**
game pattern **114**
games, classification of **114**
games, downloadable **115**
games, online **115**
Gestalt laws **140**
gesture control **55, 91**
global products **166**
GPS **19, 82, 104**
graphical element **42**
graphical user interface **18, 124**
grey scale **144**
grouping **140**

H

halo concept **91**
hand **73**

handwriting recognition **123**
hard drive **23**
hardware **65, 68, 92–93, 152**
hearing **73**
hierarchy **80–82, 85–87, 125**
hierarchy levels **78**
hierarchy, shallow **86**
hierarchy, steep **87**
highlighting **121**
hinting **137**
horizontal scrolling **34, 122**
horizontal tabs **32**
household appliances **92–93**
HSDPA **105**
human perception **73, 143, 155**

I

icon **77, 108, 119, 124–127, 130–133, 148, 152**
icon, active/inactive/selected **127**
icon alphabet **124, 131**
icon design **125, 130–131, 136**
icon size **126, 130, 136**
icon states **127, 130**
image language **132–133**
i-mode **20, 104**
inch **45**
individualisation **108**
information **80–81, 97, 140**
information architecture **159**
infrared **104**
instant feedback **60**
interaction **71, 98, 108, 113, 126**
interaction concept **76, 158**
interaction dialogue **56**
interaction techniques **60**
interaction, indirect **127**
interaction, one-handed **35, 51, 66, 71**
interaction, physical **50–73, 164–165**
interaction, two-handed **51**
interactive demonstrator **159**
interactive elements **158**
interactive guide **163**
interdisciplinary team **158, 166**
interface **30**
interface elements **160, 162**
internet **17, 25, 105, 112**
internet explorer **38**
intrinsic brightness **121, 144**
iPod **21, 53, 68**
italic **121**

J

JAVA **104**
jogdial **52, 127**
joystick **53**

K

kerning **137**
key **57, 123, 164–166**
keyboard **58–59, 66–67, 71**
keypad **58–59, 66–67, 71**
keyword **56**

kinesthetic sense **73**

L

landline connections **24**
landscape format **34**
language **118, 166**
large structures **76–93**
law of closure **141**
law of continuity **143**
law of figure/ground **142, 145**
law of good form **141**
law of proximity **140**
law of similarity **140**
law of symmetry **142**
layers **160**
layout **96, 140–143, 160, 166**
lazy-battery effect **26**
LCD **17, 154**
LCD calculator **17**
LCD, transmissive/reflective/transflective **47**
leading **137**
leafing **35**
learning **77**
learning experience **63**
learning phase **64**
legibility **118–121, 128–129, 134–135, 144, 146–147**
letter spacing **121, 128**
Li-Ion **27**
Li-Polymer **27**
line spacing **121**
list **35, 78, 96, 122**
loading bar **79**
loading speed **79**
loading time **60**
local data **96**
location **80–82, 103**
location-based services **82, 89, 102–103**
logic of games **108**
look-and-feel **159**
LPI **43**

M

machine code **92–93**
Magic cap **19**
Magic link **19**
magnification **36**
manual skill **35**
mapping **83**
meaning context **85, 88, 124**
measurement **42, 44**
memory effect **26**
mental model **82–83, 85, 87, 166–167**
menu **56**
metaphor **76–77, 88–89, 96, 124, 131**
metaphor, enclosing **77, 89**
Microsoft windows **22**
mini joystick **32, 52**
mini keyboard **25**
mini website **39**
miniaturisation **16, 24, 71**
mobile guide **150**
mobile online portfolio **39**
mobile phone **92–93**
Moore's law **24**

motion **109**
motion blur **41**
motion sensor **23, 108**
motivation **114**
motor memory **60, 63**
motor skill **50, 73**
movie **109, 111, 162**
mp3 **20**
multimedia guide **162**
multimedia interface **164–165**
multirow tabs **32**

N

natural mapping **60–62**
navigation **32, 34, 36–37, 52, 54, 56, 86–87, 90–91, 125, 148, 152**
navigation elements **120**
navigation level **86, 87**
navigation structure **96, 158, 160, 163**
navigation system **25, 39, 118, 149, 151, 164–165**
navigation zone **37, 83**
nested lists **78**
nested menu **33**
network **96–105, 112**
network products **101**
neuropointer **22**
Newton MessagePad 100 **19**
N-Gage **22**
NiCd **26**
night mode **118**
NiMh **26**
Nintendo DS **23**
non-proportional zoom **36**

O

OLED **21–22, 43, 47**
online games **115**
operating instructions **76**
operating system **92–93, 168**
organisation **80–85, 97**
organisational diagram **159, 161, 163, 166**
orientation **76**
output device **98, 134–135**
output masks **98**
output media **98**
overview **36**

P

Pacman **113**
pager **16**
palm pilot **20**
panning **34**
paper computer **158, 160**
paper prototype **169**
PC **18, 92–93**
PDA **18, 25, 55, 58, 92–93**
perception, human **73, 143, 155**
perception, visual **140**
performance **26–27**
peripheral attention **63**
peripheral use **54, 63, 73, 109, 118, 120, 140**

personalisation **108**
personal computer **18, 92–93**
perspective view **91**
phone contract **25**
physical control **62**
physical interaction **50–73, 164–165**
physical movement **70**
physical size **42, 44, 65, 127**
picture format **137**
pixel **44, 134–136**
pixel font **128, 134–135**
pixel, distorted **167**
planning **158–159**
plausible reaction **62, 143**
Playstation portable **23**
pocket pc **25, 54, 77**
point **134–135**
pop-up menu **32–33, 142**
portable computer **18**
post processing **111**
PPI **43**
presentation **159, 160, 168**
priority **161**
programming language **92–93**
proportional scroll bar **34**
proportional zoom **36**
prototyping **158**
pull-down menu **32–33, 35, 142**
PulseTouch **69**
px **43**
Pythagoras's theorem **42**

R

radio **16, 100**
reaction **60**
reading direction **61, 84**
rechargeable battery **27**
redundancy **79–81, 52, 124**
remote control **101**
resolution **42, 44–45, 119, 127, 131, 134–135, 153, 158, 160**
response time **60**
RGB **144**
rich text messages **110**
road map **83**
roaming **104**
rods **155**
rotate-and-press **58**
rotation **58, 62, 68, 164–165**

S

sample layout **160, 162, 167**
saturation **145–147, 149**
scalable concept **96**
scale function **31**
scenario **158**
screen depth **142, 145**
screen format **45, 66, 109, 122, 167**
screen location **83**
screen proportion **45, 66, 109, 122, 167**
screen size **44–45, 98, 158**
scroll bar **34, 61, 96**
scroll bar, proportional **34**
scroll wheel **52, 127, 164–165**

scrolling **35, 37**
scrolling, horizontal **34, 122**
scrolling, vertical **34, 38, 122**
search criteria **103**
selection principle **84**
semantic grouping **141**
semantic zoom **123**
semantics **61**
senses **73**
sensory perception **73**
service ideas **102**
Shockley, William **16**
sight **73**
simulation **158, 160, 164–165, 168**
simulation techniques **159**
simultaneous contrast **146**
Sinclair **18**
size **50, 58**
skins **148**
small websites **150**
smart phone **20, 25, 92–93, 98**
smart products **101**
smell **73**
smoothing **134–136**
SMS **19**
soft key **57, 64–65**
software **65, 68, 92–93, 152**
software prototype **168**
SOLED **47**
sound **71, 109**
spatial information **90–91**
spatial memory **83**
spatial order **145**
spectrum **155**
split view **91**
stand-by time **26**
static **109**
streetmap **39**
stylus **25, 35, 55, 126**
surroundings **54, 63, 73, 109, 118, 120, 140**
symbol **77**
symbolic action **70, 76, 124**
synchronous optical perception **30**
synchronous visualisation **86, 89**

T

T9 **57**
table **88**
tabs **32, 53, 126, 160**
tactile feedback **53, 69, 72**
tactile quality **53**
tamagotchi **20**
target group **108**
taste **73**
technical implementation **159**
telephone, invention of **16**
telephone keypad **57**
television **21, 100–101**
Tetris **112**
text **155**
text and contrast **118**
text display **129**
text format **137**
text input **57–59, 66, 68, 123, 129, 132–133**
TFT **21, 43**

thumbnail **41, 78**
tilting interface **70, 113**
time **80–81**
time sequence **84**
time-based location **89**
time-based organisation **88**
title bar **31**
tool **68**
touch **73**
touch sensitive **69**
touch tone **17**
touchpad **54, 67**
touchscreen **25, 54, 71, 123, 127, 166**
touchscreen technologies **72**
tracking **137**
transistor **16, 24**
transmission speed **19, 21, 108**
type **118–123**
type size **119, 120, 122, 128, 134–135**

U

UMTS **22, 105**
usability **162**
usability testing **166**
usage scenario **96, 98, 160, 169**
use **50, 54**
user acceptance **25**
user attention **142, 146**
user behaviour **85**
user expectation **83, 166**
user experience **53, 76**
user friendliness **64, 150**
user frustration **60**
user guidance **99**
user illusion **76**
user interaction **143**
user mood **111**
user needs **102**
user participation **110–111**
user preference **152**
user priority **87**
user profile **85**
user spending **115**

V

vector file **137**
vector shape **136**
vertical scrolling **34, 38, 122**
vibration **73**
virtual keyboard **59, 123**
virtual keypad **65**
virtual reality **51**
virtual representation **62**
virtual traffic signs **91**
visual perception **140**
visualisation **76, 159**
voice input **56**
voice output **56**
von Neuman, John **16**

W

walkie-talkie **16**
Walkman **18**

WAP **90, 104**
warning **143**
watch **101, 151**
wave length **155**
WCDMA **105**
website **40**
weight **26**
WiFi **104**
window **31, 35, 141, 142**
windows mobile **38**
WLAN **104**
word spacing **121**
written text **118**
WWAN **105**

X

XML **105**

Y

Yellow **144, 149**

Z

Zaurus **22**
zinc-air **27**
zoom **36, 41, 55, 88, 109, 123, 129**
zoom, disproportional **36**
zoom, flip **36**
zoom, non-proportional **36**
zoom, semantic **123**
Zuse Z1 **16**

Small is Beautiful	1A	B	16–23
	1C	24–27
The Screen	2A	30–37
	2B	38–41
	2C	42–47
Physical Interaction	3A	50–63
	3B	64–71
	3C	72–73
Large Structures on Small Screens	4A	76–87
	4B	88–91
	4C	92–93
The Network on Small Screens	5A	96–99
	5B	100–103
	5C	104–105
Entertainment on Small Screens	6A	108–109
	6B	110–113
	6C	114–115
Digital Hieroglyphs: Text and Icons on Small Screens	7A	118–127
	7B	128–133
	7C	134–137
Layout and Colour on Small Screens	8A	138–147
	8B	148–153
	8C	154–155
Developing Designs for Small Screens	9A	158–159
	9B	160–167
	9C	168–169

Brian Morris: for being an ever challenging publisher.

Caroline Walmsley: for being our editor. The reward is in the result.

Victor Dewsbury: for beautifully capturing our train of thought and casting it in elegant English.

A special thanks goes to **Tomoko Obana**. She looked into Japan and thus into the future for us, without her the book would have not been possible in this form.

Claudia Dallendörfer contributed as our project scout in California – thank you.

Gerhard Mauter: his diligence and precision with the observation and development of man-machine interfaces never cease to impress us.

Christian Langer: his experience and his enthusiasm with the development of mobile applications were a major contribution to this book. We owe him a special thanks for his description of the development for the mobile guides for Marwell Zoo.

Christine Strothotte: for her crystal-clear intellect and her help in clarifying basic concepts in computer science. Thank you for being such an insightful partner at the University of Applied sciences in Magdeburg.

Robert Laux: for your patience and inspiration over the last five years.

Reik Wendt und Matthias Schröder: for designing Alice the pixel font.

Aaron Marcus: for coining the phrase 'babyface'.

Patrick Baudisch: for his inspiring concepts and his openness to share them with us and the world.

Maic Masuch: for his book recommendations.

Florian Petri: he was not afraid to take the part of the Homunculus.

Giesela Kasten: for her expert knowledge in the field of perception.

Nick Roericht: for inspiring material.

We would like to thank our colleagues and the faculty members at the **University of Applied Science in Magdeburg** and at the **University of the Arts in Berlin** for their support and understanding during the making of the book.

For their exemplary projects:
Hendrik Rieß
Anna Zesewitz
Anne Grüngreiff
Katharina Schlosser
Susanne Stage
Zhang Chao
Franziska Langbrandtner
Julia Ellrich
Alexander Gessler
Johannes Köpp
Volker Kaufmann

...and all at **studio 7.5**: for being so patient and supportive and making it happen once again ;)

Carola Zwick, Burkhard Schmitz and Kerstin Kühl
June 2005